MW00325289

Table of Contents

Preface

"Humor is man's affirmation of dignity, His declaration of superiority over all that may befall him."
—Romaine Gary

A man is involved in a motor vehicle accident and suffers a broken leg, a broken arm, internal injuries, and multiple cuts and bruises. He is taken to a hospital emergency room where a doctor asks him, "Do you have any pain?" and the man replies, "Only when I laugh!" This story illustrates mankind's indomitable spirit and capacity for humor even in the direst of circumstances. As a physician for over forty years, I never cease to be delighted at the humorous side of my patients and the medical community in general. Even when chronically ill, patients come up with some amusing stories, anecdotes, quips, one-liners, and humor in general. Even when I find myself in medically tense situations, humor springs forth to lighten the day, either at the time or in retrospect.

Most physicians use humor to ease the psychological burden of caring for critically ill and sometimes terminally ill patients. I began collecting this material when I was in medical school at the University of Virginia, but it spans my forty-plus years of medical practice, including my postgraduate years at Norfolk General Hospital in Norfolk, Virginia, my United States Air Force career from 1970 to 1972 in Kenai, Alaska, and later my private practice in Wytheville, Virginia, where I have been since 1973. I have kept these stories on scraps of paper in a burgeoning file in my office, awaiting a time when I might publish them for the edification and pleasure of other people, and in January of 2008, with my partial retirement, the time finally arrived.

Over the years I have collected literally hundreds of examples of medically related humor, ranging from mispronunciation of medical terms to detailed stories and anecdotes. The material presented here is primarily from my own experience with patients, but some has come from my colleagues, who, knowing of my interest, have related to me their own stories. It is not unusual for a physician or a nurse to pull me aside with the explanation, "Have I got one for you!" In the hustle and bustle of everyday practice, I have sometimes forgotten the origin of the story, but where memory serves, I have named names and places because, ultimately, this book is about people, people with names, and faces, and personalities, and it seems appropriate for me to connect the people with their stories. As I reread each anecdote from the folder, the memory of that person comes flooding back, and I chuckle in remembrance of when I first heard the story. I felt that writing these stories anonymously would detract from the personality of the book; however, where a story might be an embarrassment to the teller, I have written it without the name or changed the name. I have told the majority of my contributors that I intended to include their stories and, to a person, they agreed that it would be a privilege to have their stories included. For those whom I have not asked, I suspect they will also get pleasure from knowing they have contributed a little to lightening the world's burdens with their humor.

For readers who know few or none of these folks, that will not detract from the inherent humor of the story, but for those thousands of people whose lives have been touched by the characters in the book, as they read these stories they will nod their heads and say to themselves, "Isn't that just like old so-and-so?" and again, the personality of the person is revealed through the stories.

Over the years here, my wife, Mimi, and I have been fortunate to raise a daughter, Margaret, who has a PhD in public health and who teaches at Radford University in Radford, Virginia, and a son, James

Judson IV, who is a gynecologist in Winter Haven, Florida. It is to these three people that I owe my happiness and my success, and it is they who have made it possible for me to live long enough to write these stories. I dedicate this book to them and hope that they may read one or two stories here that I have not already told them many times.

I would also like to recognize my partners, my nurses, my laboratory technicians, and my support staff who are mentioned so many times in this book and who have made the practice of medicine a pleasure instead of a "job." My great uncle, Robert E. Booker, M.D., a long-deceased country doctor, once told me that he had never worked a day in his life. It is because of my fellow physicians and my nurses that I can make that same statement. Thank you all for a life that could not get much better.

I have thought of many titles for this book, but all seem unimaginative or poorly descriptive. The catchy title comes from Joe, whom I hospitalized many years ago with a stomach ulcer which had bled profusely and from which he nearly died. It was days before he was able to even think of food, and I was beginning to think I would have to insert a nasogastric tube through his nose and into his stomach to give him adequate nourishment. It was, then, to my great relief that one morning when I made rounds he told me "Doc, I'm so hungry I could eat ham, lamb, ram, bull, beef, and bear." Here's to Joe; wherever he is, I hope he's sated.

Humor and Health

Anyone who has heard a baby laugh needs no convincing that this is innate behavior, but there is a large body of scientific evidence to indicate that laughter is a genetic trait in human beings. In addition to making our lives more fun, laughter has other salutary effects, including protection from disease. Our bodies have many complex disease-fighting systems, and our ability to appreciate humor and to laugh seems to be one of these. There are systems that act directly on the offending attacker, and there are systems that serve to activate the primary systems. Laughter falls into the latter category, and it has long been known that people who have a positive outlook on life, and who approach life with an optimistic attitude seem to enjoy better health than negative people. Dr. Franz Ingelfinger, a past editor of the prestigious *New England Journal of Medicine,* reasoned that our bodies possess the ability to heal over 85% of all human illness, and Dr. Norman Vincent Peale wrote about *The Power of Positive Thinking.* We are now beginning to see how these factors are interrelated.

Psychoneuroimmunology is the field of study that deals with the mind/body connection and how our emotions and outlook on life affect the immune system and its defense capabilities. Studies have shown that laughter, which is both psychological and physiological, has multiple positive effects on our sense of well-being and our ability to fight disease.

Muscle Relaxation

Most people will say that a good, hearty laugh always leaves them feeling relaxed and positive. This has been confirmed with bio-feedback studies, which show patients are much more relaxed after watching humorous videos than after watching non-humorous material. One hilarious scene in the movie *The Bucket List,* starring Morgan Freeman and Jack Nicholson, shows them crossing off one item on their list of things to do before kicking the bucket by laughing until they are both crying. Afterwards, the scene shows them more relaxed and at ease, with the tension of the moment dissipated.

Cardiovascular Conditioning

Have you ever noticed that you feel refreshingly fatigued after vigorous laughing? It is because laughing is actually aerobic exercise. Researchers have estimated that hearty laughing 100 times is equivalent to 15 minutes of moderate exertion on an exercise bike. Laughing increases blood flow, increases oxygenation of the blood, exercises the diaphragm and abdominal muscles, and probably contributes to lowered blood pressure.

Reduction of Stress Hormones

One of my partners, Dr. Wayne Horney, commented frequently that if he were going to get sick, it would be after a weekend on call for our large, seven-person call group. He was convinced that the stress lowered his immunity and allowed a virus to take hold. There is research to support his contention, and it revolves about the decline in disease resistance induced by stress.

When we are faced with a dangerous situation, "fight or flight" hormones are released into the bloodstream. These hormones prepare us to either fight the danger or to run from it, thus the term, "fight or flight." Stress engenders the same response with the release of those hormones called epinephrine, cortisol, dopamine, and growth hormone. In a true "fight or flight" situation, this reaction is beneficial, but under stress, which is longer in duration, it is detrimental and results in hypertension, depression, anxiety, vascular disease, and a reduction in serum antibodies. Studies show that laughter and the appreciation of humor reduces these hormones and lessens their effects.

Immunity Enhancement

There are two basic types of immunity, humoral, which is antibody based, and cellular, which resides with defensive cell activity. Lessening of humoral immunity may also have contributed to Dr. Horney's post-weekend viral illness. It is well known that various antibodies protect us from infections such as viruses, bacteria, fungi, and parasites. This is the function of five different antibodies termed "immunoglobulins," which we represent as IgA, IgD, IgE, IgG, and IgM. They each address a different area of immunity, but it appears that all are enhanced by humor and laughter. Most research has been done on IgA, which is found in the mucous secretions of the respiratory and digestive tracts, and which protects us from infectious diseases in these systems. It is also present in colostrum, which appears in breast milk during the first two or three days after delivery and is important in the transfer of passive antibodies from mother to child. Several studies have shown a significant increase of IgA in saliva and blood after watching humorous videos, and this occurs in both children and adults. In addition, IgM, IgG, and another humoral chemical known as complement have also been shown to increase with laughter.

Cellular immunity is also enhanced by watching comedy videos. B cells are produced in bone marrow and, although they do not directly attack invaders, they produce the antibodies used in humoral immunity. These cells "recognize" invaders known as "antigens" and produce antibodies specific for destroying them. They also have the capacity for "remembering" the antigen and then circulate in the blood in anticipation of the antigen appearing again, at which time they respond much more quickly in producing the appropriate antibody to destroy the invader.

13

T cells are another type of defense mechanism and operate differently from the B cells. They directly interact with the invader and elicit killer responses from other cells known as lymphocytes and leukocytes, which belong in the category of white blood cells. The T cells have also been shown to increase in response to laughter.

In addition to its effect on B cells, antibodies, complement, and T cells, laughter also increases the amount of gamma interferon, a protein which enhances the function of both B cells and T cells, where it serves to activate and regulate defensive cellular activity.

It appears then that there is a very close relationship between humor, laughter, and a lighthearted approach to life that stimulates various parts of our very complex immune system. This operates through the psychoneuroimmunology system, and we can take advantage of this in several ways. First, there is no shortage of humorous television shows, movies, videos, and comedy clubs to get you laughing. Avoid the edge-of-your-seat thriller; get a comedy and laugh for an hour or two. Second, join with your family and friends in humorous settings. Laughter is contagious; whenever everyone else is rolling in the aisles, it is hard not to join in. And finally, find humor in your life. It is all around you just waiting to be discovered. Turn anger and frustration into laughter by finding a way to see it humorously.

As I have said, the impetus for this book came primarily from patients, who even though they were ill, found time for laughter and humor and especially to share it with others. Instead of complaining and grousing about their misfortune, they chose to see it with levity, as did Danny Cressell, who was so dizzy with inner ear dysfunction he could hardly stand up, but joked with me that his "wiggling pin had come out of his wobbling shaft!" To the Dannys of the world, may their tribe increase!

The Medical School Years

Because the majority of material in this book consists of brief non-related stories and does not have to be read in any order, I have elected to organize it in approximate chronological order beginning in medical school at the University of Virginia and proceeding up to the present, March 2008. As I have indicated, I began this collection during my first year in medical school in June 1963, so the stories in this chapter begin from that year and go through to my last year there. Subsequent chapters will detail later years in my career and will be annotated in those sections.

The Adventures of Bill

Patients have no corner on the humor market, and physicians have their own brand of humor, some of which can be written. Gross anatomy was one of the first subjects we took as first-year medical students and, despite the rather gruesome nature of dissecting human cadavers, there was a great deal of opportunity for tomfoolery. Bill was a member of my first-year class at the University of Virginia, although unfortunately, he did not make it to the second. Despite his short tenure, he provided a great deal of levity both intentional and otherwise that first year. It began with George nearly falling off his dissecting stool when his cadaver's arm suddenly flopped up beside his head. He had failed to see the fine fishing string attached to the arm and going up over the old fluorescent light fixture to Bill's side of the table. For the next few weeks various parts of the cadavers became animated under Bill's skillful maneuvering, but by the time the penis on Vivian's cadaver suddenly became erect, she had learned enough that, without missing a dissecting beat, she cut the string with a deft flip of the dissecting knife. And her subsequent withering glare at Bill put an end to the mysteriously animated cadaver parts.

As we moved through our dissections, we eventually came to the gastrointestinal tract, and one of our projects was to remove the small intestine, which can be over thirty feet long. We were to open the entire length, wash out the contents into the old utility-type sinks, and then examine the inside for evidence of disease, deformity, prior surgery, etc. As Bill was completing this task, an end of the intestine slipped down the drain hole. There was opportunity here! And Bill began to feed the gut down the drain inch by inch and foot by foot. As the rest of us learned what was going on, we gathered around his sink to see if he could, indeed, get the entire length down the drain and speculated on where the other end would be. Suddenly, an ominous silence spread from the back of the class toward the sink as the anatomy professor had heard the commotion and had come to investigate. We innocent bystanders silently melted away to our tables and surreptitiously watched as the professor oversaw Bill slowly pull the thirty-plus feet of intestine out of the netherworld of the drainpipe, inch by inch and foot by foot. Not a word was spoken during this agonizingly long process and when it was all out, the professor left the room, again without saying a word. Bill later told us that had been the loudest silence he had ever heard!

Second semester brought physiology (the study of how the body works) to our budding medical world. In those days, we were our own guinea pigs, and numerous experiments about how the human body works were performed using ourselves as subjects. One such demonstration involved the study of the respiratory tract and the effect of various gases in the atmosphere on that system. The air we breathe is about 80% nitrogen and 20% oxygen, with minute percentages of other gases thrown in for good measure. We inhale this mixture and breathe out almost the same combination but with some carbon dioxide from our lungs mixed in. We used Douglas bags, large canvas-covered rubber bags, to collect different gasses from large cylinders in the center of the room. Through special mouth pieces, we allowed our subject, Bill, to breathe these different gasses and mixtures thereof and recorded his vital signs and other observations, such as skin color, eye reactions, alertness, etc. One part of the protocol required him to breathe pure nitrogen for a short time and then switch him to pure oxygen to wash out the nitrogen. Unfortunately, George, our guy in charge of the bags, got them mixed up and we put poor Bill on pure carbon dioxide by mistake. Needless to say, Bill got only a few breaths down before he fainted dead away and was saved from the floor only by George's quick reflexes! We found this funny only in retrospect.

The Silver Fox

Dr. Wilbur Pardon was our professor for *Introduction to Medicine*, a class designed to teach the rudiments of patient interviewing, history taking, physical examination, and disease evaluation. He was a tall, slim man with silver-white hair, and a regal bearing, who was known as "the Silver Fox." His interviewing skills were legendary, and we looked forward to seeing him demonstrate his approach to patients. Unfortunately, the first patient he interviewed for us was a man whose answering skills were equal to Dr. Pardon's' interviewing skills. This fellow worked as a truck driver for a company logging the mountains around Charlottesville. He had developed a bleeding duodenal ulcer, and wound up a patient on the medical ward. Dr. Pardon started out by eliciting some background about the logging business and said, "I suspect the logging business has gotten easier with chainsaws, hasn't it?"

"Yes sir, I guess you could say that."

"It's easier than using those old cross-cut saws, isn't it?"

"Yes, sir, it is that."

"And it just takes one man to operate one, doesn't it?"

"Well, yes sir, it just takes one man, but boss, it takes a man." His emphasis on "it takes a man" brought he house down, and Dr. Pardon could only smile.

As the interview went on, Dr. Pardon tried to tie the man's diet to the development of the ulcer, and he asked about what he ate. The man replied that he usually ate a sandwich as he drove off the mountain with a load of logs. In a conversational tone, Dr. Pardon asked him if he ever just ate pork and beans right out of the can. The fellow paused for a second, looked at Dr. Pardon and said, "Doctor, has you ever tried to eat pork and beans while you's drivin' a load of logs off Brown's Mountain?" This really did the trick, and Dr. Pardon stuck to a less risky interviewing tactic for the rest of the class.

Dr. Alman

Dr. Meriwether Alman was a general surgeon who enjoyed his reputation as a rapscallion teacher of medical students, interns, and residents. He frequently smoked cigars, and was gruff and abrupt, but we enjoyed his antics. In one session with a small group of us third-year students, he was quizzing Emmit about thyroid disease. Emmit began by talking about calcium (a parathyroid problem), whereupon Dr. Alman pounded the table with his cigar-holding hand sending sparks flying all over the place and bellowed "Hell, son, you ain't even in the right disease!"

Another Dr. Alman story came to me by way of John, who was a classmate and who was in the operating room with him during an abdominal procedure. As with many procedures in a teaching hospital, there were a number of people in the operating theater observing the process. As the operation came to a successful conclusion, Dr. Alman suddenly stood back from the table, appearing concerned and sniffed the air. Of course, everyone in the room froze waiting to see what he was doing. Addressing the surgical resident assisting on the case, he said "Richard, I smell gas...bowel gas. That can mean one of two things: either I have accidentally cut this patient's bowel or someone in this room has passed gas. If I have cut the bowel, we will have to go back in, search for the hole and sew it up, so hopefully it is the latter." He then paused and asked very seriously, "Has anyone in this room just passed gas?" In the resulting dead silence, a student nurse in the back of the room sheepishly raised her hand. At that, Dr. Alman walked out of the room saying over his shoulder, "Finish it up, Richard."

John did not know if Dr. Alman had actually smelled anything or just took a chance that he would catch someone with recently passed flatus. John was glad that he was not the culprit!

Charlie

To be called on to present a case in "the pit" was a sure way to instill fear into the soul of a fourth-year medical student. The pit was a huge amphitheater where third- and fourth-year students, interns, residents, fellows, and attending physicians gathered once a week to study, in depth, a given medical subject in a forum called, "grand rounds." Typically, a fourth-year student would be asked to present the history of a patient with that disease along with the physical exam findings, lab and x-ray results, and the patient's course in the hospital. Afterward, the student was fair game for any and all questions from the audience on any subject even remotely related to the central issue. Since the audience consisted of seasoned physicians from every discipline, it was a tense time for anyone unlucky enough to have taken care of such a patient. Charlie was the chosen student on this particular day, and he was presenting a patient who had just had a cardiac pacemaker inserted. In those days, cardiac pacemakers were a new technology and were really the hot topic in cardiology circles. Charlie was taken with the new procedure, and was sure that he would be grilled on pacemaker technology, the indications for inserting a pacemaker, the care and follow-up of a pacemaker patient, etc. Accordingly, he became our student expert on pacemakers. He studied every scrap of information he could find on pacemakers, even contacting the company which made the device, and felt like he was going to score a grandslam. Of course, all of us fourth-year students knew that he was presenting and what he had done to prepare, and we were looking forward to his being able to really wow the establishment. As luck would have it, the chairman of the department of cardiac surgery was overseeing this particular presentation. When Charlie finished presenting the basic information on the patient, the chairman said, "Mr. Peters, that was an excellent presentation. Now what can you tell us about aortic stenosis?" A deathly silence descended on the room as we awaited Charlie's response, knowing that he was not prepared for this question. When he finally began to speak, we all heaved a sigh of relief as he said, "Well, Sir, aortic stenosis is a marked narrowing of the aortic valve of the heart and is sometimes an indication for a cardiac pacemaker!" For the next half hour, Charlie held forth eloquently and educated everyone in the amphitheater about pacemakers. I don't know if the chairman was aware of what had happened, but if he did, he was a good sport and didn't let on.

The Chairman and "Dr. Booker"

Patient rounds in an academic center follow an unwritten, but invariable processional hierarchy. The undisputed head of this order is the attending physician, followed by the fellows, who are fully trained doctors honing their skills in a specific specialty, followed by the chief resident, followed by the lesser residents, followed by the interns, followed by the fourth-year medical students, followed by the lowest of the low, the third-year medical students. Ironically, it is usually the third-year medical student who spends the most face-to-face time with the patient, as he or she is required to take a detailed history, leaving out no positive and very few negative responses, do a complete physical exam, again noting both positive and negative findings; formulate a diagnosis, outline a plan of evaluation, and then execute all orders when approved by the intern or resident. In my day, we also had to draw all of the blood, take it to the lab, obtain the results, and then see that they got on the chart.

I was a third-year medical student rotating through surgery and fully immersed in the above order of things when the chairman of cardiac surgery, he of the above anecdote, came onto the floor to conduct rounds on a patient of mine who was going to have a diseased aortic valve replaced, a relatively new procedure in those days. He led the procession down the hall and stopped outside Mrs. Smith's room, where he gave a brief lecture on the patient's condition, the indications for the procedure, the details of the operation, and other elements of the planned procedure. We then trooped into the room and arranged ourselves around the bed in the same order as we came down the hall, with the third-year medical students in the very back of the room and some even out in the hall. The chairman spoke briefly to Mrs. Smith and explained to her what he planned to do and why and told her that the operation was planned for the following morning, whereupon Mrs. Smith, still in control of her destiny, stated, "I ain't going nowhere until Dr. Booker says it's all right!" A stunned silence followed, since few in the crowd even knew who I was.

The chairman looked at the fellows and asked, "Who is Dr. Booker?" The fellows, equally puzzled, looked at the residents, who looked at the interns, who looked at the fourth-year students, who looked at the third-year students, who all turned and looked at me!

Believe me, there was no hole deep enough at that moment, but I bravely willed my quaking innards to push through the crowd and approach the bed. I was aware of every eye on me as I took her hand and said, "Mrs. Smith, this operation will make you much better, and there is no one better to do this than Dr. Muller. I think you should go ahead with it."

Her answer was a simple, "Okay," and I melted back through the crowd and on into the hall as the processional proceeded to the next case. Later, as the esteemed chairman was leaving the floor, he stopped me and said, "Believe it or not, you were the most important person in that room this morning. Never forget how you got there."

All Pain Is Real

I am always amazed at how pearls of medical wisdom drop into my lap at odd times. I am not talking about the mundane knowledge of medicine, but that bit of insight that forever changes the way you practice medicine. One such pearl came to me during third-year psychiatry rounds. Several of us were presenting patients to our attending, Dr. Vincent Burgman, and Jon had a particularly troubling case which had been referred to us from the medical service. A middle-aged lady had been admitted for abdominal pain, and had been thoroughly evaluated from a physical standpoint with nothing being found to explain her pain. Psychiatry had been consulted to rule out psychological causes. Jon presented her case along with all of the lab and x-ray data, none of which identified a physical etiology, but nonetheless, Jon said, "I think her pain is real."

Dr. Burgman fixed him with a steely stare, and in mock indignation said, "Mr. Barker, all pain is real, the etiology simply guides one's therapy." Despite the humorous setting, Dr. Burgman's admonition that "All pain is real," regardless of its etiology, physical or psychological, is a constant reminder to me not to disregard a patient's complaints of pain despite my being unable to find an objective cause for that pain.

But Now I Don't Care

Dr. Burgman, of the above anecdote, gave us a lecture on tranquilizers and was talking about a newly developed French drug called Thorazine. To illustrate its effectiveness he told us of the minister of a local church who became so nervous when he preached before large congregations that he became incontinent and had to wear pads in his undershorts. After the failure of other medicine to remedy the situation, Dr. Burgman had put him on Thorazine. After several weeks, the minister returned and seemed to be very pleased with the results. "So," Dr. Burgman said, "you've quit wetting your pants?"

"Well, no," the minister replied, "I am still incontinent at times, but now I don't worry about it!"

The White Spot

"The Corner" is really not a corner at all, but anyone who has ever attended the University of Virginia knows about the corner which is not a corner. Across from the old medical school, the corner is a street along which is a collection of businesses consisting of book stores, restaurants, hole-in-the-wall eateries, a pool hall, a parking lot, and, most famously Mincer's Pipe Shop, which is not a pipe shop at all any more, but a source for UVa apparel, memorabilia, gifts, etc. "The Corner" is a favorite gathering place for UVa faithful and is the centerpiece for this next story.

I was in my final year at UVa and was on call in the emergency room on a Saturday afternoon. It had been relatively quiet as far as Saturdays go in Charlottesville, and Ken, an undergraduate student working at the admissions desk, planned to go to supper early in case it started getting busier in the evening. In the late-afternoon Ken admitted an undergraduate student with pernicious nausea, vomiting, and abdominal cramps, which appeared to be a case of viral gastroenteritis, that is, until, in quick succession, we admitted several more students with the same symptoms, and this looked like something more ominous. These folks were really ill, requiring IV fluids and IV medications, so we quickly ran out of rooms and began putting patients on stretchers in the halls. The cases appeared to be related, but we were unable to pinpoint the source.

In a lull about 5:30, Ken left for supper. While he was gone, and with a few more cases of this vile disorder, we finally discovered the common thread...hot dogs at the White Spot, a local eatery on "The Corner." When Ken returned, we proudly told him that we had solved the mystery, but instead of reveling in our successful sleuthing, he turned pale and anxious. He had just eaten two hot dogs at the White Spot! Well, food poisoning of this type usually has a delay from ingestion to symptoms of about four hours, and I can vouch for at least one incidence of that approximate timing, as it was 3 hours and 50 minutes to the first mad grab for the trash can and only a little while longer before he was on a stretcher getting IV fluids and IV Compazine, an anti-emetic frequently used in those days. Fortunately, with calls to the White Spot and to the health department, we were able to contain the cases fairly quickly. Since the illnesses were of short duration, the emergency room was back to normal by Sunday morning, and Ken recovered without complications or sequelae. Once again, out of the blue, I had another retrospectively humorous anecdote for my growing file of material for a book to written some forty years later.

Yow!

Richard was the chief resident on the TCV (Thoracic-Cardio-Vascular) surgery service during my fourth year. He was outgoing and friendly, and all of us students liked him and gathered to him when he was on the floor. His one flaw, especially for one in his position, was that he smoked; unfiltered Camels, no less! We were well aware of his habit, but in those days there was no stringent prohibition on smoking in the hospital, and we accepted him, habit and all.

One day we got on the elevator on the sixth floor of the hospital with several other folks, one of whom was smoking, and Dick lit up one of his Camels. As luck would have it, the elevator stopped on the fourth floor and who should get on but Dr. Kanton Drate and Dr. Gregory Mirrow, both TCV surgeons and professors, and both with violent anti-smoking biases. We were in the back of the elevator, and the smell of cigarette smoke could be attributed to the other person smoking, but Dick had nowhere to extinguish the weed. He wound up cupping it into his hand and sticking it into his jacket pocket, awaiting the departure of the professors, hopefully on one of the next floors. No such luck! They rode to the first floor and got out only to continue their discussion right outside of the elevator. Dick obviously planned to ride on back to another floor, but they caught sight of him, and Dr. Mirrow called out "Oh, Dick, may we see you a moment?" This was too good to pass up, so four or five of us students exited with him, and though we wandered down the hall a ways, we stayed well within sight of this drama being played out.

It was obvious that Dick was as nervous as a long-tailed cat in a room full of rocking chairs, and he made several discussion-ending statements, but the professors were intent on their mission and would not let him off the hook. Eventually, the burning Camel reached the end and Dick jerked his hand out of the pocket and flung the still smoldering tip on the floor. Both Dr. Drate's and Dr. Mirrow's startled looks instantly turned to incredulity, and Dick's reputation took a nosedive, as both professors turned on their collective heels and left Dick in their wake, Dr. Mirrow throwing over his shoulder, "Richard, I am extremely disappointed; I expect better from my residents!"

I don't know if Dick stopped smoking, but that would surely have been impetus enough for most of us to have done so.

Look at the Light

One of our first experiences with chronic illness came in our second year on a field trip to the state hospital in Staunton, Virginia, where we saw illnesses that are now a thing of the past. One such patient was a woman whose skin was a striking silvery-grey color due to her long-term use of silver-containing nose drops (thankfully, no longer made), the silver having been deposited in her skin. The patients were in their rooms, and outside the door was a summary of their condition and the attendant physical findings. One of our instructors was Dr. S., a pathologist, whose clinical skills with living beings were a little rusty. He led our group into a patient's room after reading us the summary describing an unusual problem of the eyes called retinitis pigmentosa where the retina of the eye is black. Dr. S.'s pathology background gave him a excellent knowledge of what the condition entailed, and as he held the opthalmoscope to his eye he described what he "saw" in great detail. I was impressed with his opthalmoscopic abilities until Richard whispered in my ear, "Look on his forehead!" I moved a little toward Richard and peered over at Dr. S,, where I saw the light of the instrument, shining not in the patient's eye, but on Dr. S.'s forehead! Memory, not visualization was the key to his excellent description of the eye findings!

Where's the Toilet?

The physiology test was the next day, and Bill and I were in the lab studying. The hour was late, and we still had a lot of material to review. I was doing pretty well, but Bill was about at the end of his rope sleepwise. He kept dozing off and was getting further behind. He asked me if I had anything that he could take to stay awake. I was not in the habit of taking alertness drugs, but had a box of Vivarin in my case. The label said that it had 200 mg of caffeine in each pill (a seven-ounce cup of coffee has about 175 mg) so Bill took five of them. In about thirty minutes his alertness had increased, but his bladder capacity seemingly had decreased. He was running to the toilet every ten to fifteen minutes, and by his account, "I'm peeing myself to death!" We wondered why he was doing this, and if the caffeine had anything to do with it since he had taken so many pills. The answer did not come to us until the following year when we took pharmacology and were studying "psychoactive chemicals," one of which is caffeine. Our textbook had this to say, "Caffeine—a bitter white crystalline xanthine that acts like a stimulant and a diuretic." Case solved!

Hair In, Hair Out

The ear has three separate divisions, including external, middle, and internal components. The idea that the external ear had no effect on the internal mechanism was dispelled one day when I was working in the ear-nose-throat clinic. A middle-aged man was brought into the clinic by some friends when he had become extremely dizzy while getting a haircut over on the corner. He had been perfectly fine going into the barber shop, but as barber had been using a blower to remove the hair from his collar, he became so dizzy he could not stand without help.

We helped him into the examining chair and the resident examined him thoroughly, but could find nothing of great significance except that he had a piece of hair leaning against the eardrum. He reached into the canal with a pair of forceps and removed the hair. Immediately, the man said, "Gosh, it's gone…the dizziness is gone!" Well, we were astonished at the assumption that the hair could have caused the dizziness, so the resident put the hair back against the eardrum and the dizziness immediately returned. This was such an unusual finding that for the next half hour, every attending, fellow, resident, intern and medical student in ENT clinic had to witness the hair in and hair out phenomenon. Finally, Dr. Fitzhugh, the chairman of the department, took pity on the poor man and called a halt to the exhibitions, but from then on we were all convinced that there is certainly a connection between the external and internal ear despite being separated by the middle.

All Aboard, Thunk!

This story comes from our anatomy professor as he was describing the function of the carotid sinus, a blood-pressure regulator in the carotid artery in the neck at the angle of the jaw. Baroreceptors govern the level of blood pressure by constantly adjusting the pressure to keep it in the right range. As the heart beats, these receptors register the pressure in the artery, and if it is too high, the receptor signals the cardiovascular system to lower the pressure and, conversely, if the pressure is too low, it will signal the system to raise the pressure. Some people have very sensitive carotid sinus baroreceptors, which will even register external pressure on the neck as an increase in blood pressure and drop the blood pressure accordingly. In severe cases, it may even cause fainting, which brings us to the gist of the story.

A middle-aged man presented in the medical clinic with a complaint of "fainting." Further questioning revealed that he was a conductor on a Norfolk and Western passenger train, and that he almost always had the fainting spells at work. As the train was getting ready to leave the station, he would lean out of the car and, looking both ways for late passengers, he would call "All Aboard." It was during this time that he would faint. The physicians in the clinic were intrigued and had him repeat the stated maneuver over and over in the clinic, but without a hint of fainting. Being very curious and frustrated, one of the resident physicians volunteered to go with the conductor on one of this runs to see if he could spot the problem. On the appointed day, the conductor showed up all decked out in his black and white uniform even down to a new celluloid collar. The resident trailed the conductor as he went about his duties and was standing right behind him as the train was set to depart. The conductor leaned out of the train, looked to the left and yelled, "All Aboard." He then looked to the right and yelled, "All…" and promptly passed out on the platform!

Enlightenment is a wonderful thing, and the resident immediately diagnosed the problem. As the conductor turned his head to the right, the stiff celluloid collar pushed up under the angle of the jaw, compressed the carotid sinus, which dropped the blood pressure, dropped the pulse rate, and dropped the conductor…onto the platform! The solution was simple and effective, but essentially non-medical: the conductor exchanged his stiff celluloid collar for a soft cotton one.

There is nothing more satisfying to a physician than to unravel a convoluted diagnostic conundrum and come up with right answer, especially if it has befuddled many of his fellow physicians. I suspect the resident lost no opportunities to remind his fellows of his coup!

B-o-r-i-n-g …

Pharmacology was one of the most boring of our medical classes. It was here we studied the actions of literally hundreds of drugs, and, in short order, our brains were a mish-mash of effects, side-effects, idiosyncrasies, black-box warnings, reactions, interactions, etc. It was especially bad that one of the professors talked to his feet in a monotone that never varied more than one-fourth of an octave. Such was the situation with Dr. B., who draped himself over the lectern, resting his forearms and one foot on it and proceeded to drone on and on, describing one drug after another in minute detail. The level of boredom could be gauged by the number of students who were either mesmerized or asleep, but we did not realize the degree of lethargy until there came an unnatural pause in the drone, and when we looked up, Dr. B. was fast asleep as well…was even snoring! We watched in amazement for perhaps thirty to forty-five seconds when he suddenly shook himself awake, reoriented himself and continued the lecture!

It was not until later that we discovered that Dr. B. had narcolepsy, and these spells were not uncommon for him. He had even chosen pharmacology as a career because it allowed him to search for an effective treatment or cure for narcolepsy. In retrospect, the spell had an unexpected outcome, in that whenever Dr. B. lectured, everyone was wide awake, alert, and concentrating on the lecture as, no one wanted to miss a repeat performance!

Yuck!

This story came to me by way of an old country doctor while I was taking physiology at the University of Virginia. It had actually happened to him when he was taking physiology at the Medical College of Virginia. The topic was diabetes mellitus, which the professor explained was a term derived from Greek and Latin and meant "the passing of honey-sweet urine" because of the presence of glucose in the urine of diabetics. To illustrate his point, he produced a container of urine from a diabetic whose sugar was quite high. He dipped his finger into the container and tasted the urine. He then passed the container among the medical students who dutifully tasted the urine and subsequently confirmed its sweetness. When the container returned to the front of the room, the professor proceeded to tell the class that had they been alert, they would have noticed that he dipped his forefinger into the urine, but tasted his middle finger! Not a few of the students were noted to be spitting vigorously into their handkerchiefs!

Pigeons

Much has transpired since I graduated from medical school at the University of Virginia, including building a new medical school. Many of us older physicians viewed the move with nostalgia, for the old building is so typical Jeffersonian. The entrance is a magnificent edifice fronted by a broad portico whose columns support an impressive roof. The eave under the roof is inset above a wide stone ledge which pigeons find accommodating, as they have a protected resting place out of the wind and rain and other assaults of nature. Attempts to displace the pigeons have been unsuccessful without destroying the appearance of the building, which is so much a part of the panache of the facade, and so they congregate there in profusion. The building is entered from a flagstone terrace bordered by low balustrades, upon which many of us were sitting on a warm, sunny noon-hour break just days before we were to graduate. As we were rejoicing in having survived the rigors of a medical education, a young man approached Richard and asked directions to the dean's office. Richard assumed that he was applying to medical school, which the young man affirmed. Richard proceeded to tell him about the difficulty of the courses, the endless hours of lectures, the interminable hours of study, the grilling by the professors, the tongue lashing by the interns and residents, etc., etc., and then asked him if he still wanted to endure such indignities. When the young man replied that he was certain he could endure, Richard waxed eloquent and said there was one other aspect to consider, "Behold the pigeons on yon ledge. If you are accepted, the dean's secretary will assign you a special bird, and every day for the first two years, as you enter these hallowed halls, that pigeon will defecate upon your head and, as a mark of privilege, you will be required to wear that badge for the rest of the day." The young man obviously knew that Richard was putting him on, but we also noted with amusement that, as he entered the building, he carefully chose a path between pigeons!

The Postgraduate Years

After graduation from the University of Virginia, my future partner, Dr. James B. Stone, III, and I began our subsequent training at Norfolk General Hospital in Norfolk, Virginia. We had chosen this center because of its reputation for producing family physicians well trained to care for the full spectrum of human illness from the cradle to the grave. This training was a coordinated three-year program, including pediatrics, internal medicine and its subspecialties, surgery and its subspecialties, obstetrics and gynecology, and geriatrics. Our mode of practice and our success in the field of medicine is a tribute to the excellent training there. Interestingly, at the time, the postgraduate training program was in transition from simply a large city hospital to one associated with a new medical school, which was to be known as Eastern Virginia Medical School. The new teaching staff was being assembled, and many of our attending physicians would later become professors in the new medical school, so in a very real sense, we had the best of both worlds. We had the atmosphere of a large city hospital, where we had the freedom to pursue our own course, and we had the embryonic academic atmosphere with the structure of a true medical school. We came out the winners in ways that the training of modern family physicians does not match, but that is fodder for another book.

The stories in this chapter all come from my experiences at Norfolk General Hospital from 1968 to 1970 and from 1972 to 1973, with the intervening years from 1970 to 1972 being spent in the United States Air Force, which will be the subject of the next chapter.

The Page System

As Norfolk General Hospital prepared to become part of the Eastern Virginia Medical School, the administration sought to expand its cadre of well-trained native English-speaking interns and residents. They found their medical mother lode in Scotland and Ireland, and there were a number of Scotch and Irish physicians in my internship class. These fellows got their doctorates in a coordinated six-year program, whereas we Americans had separate four years of undergraduate school and four years of medical school. From a practical standpoint, these physicians were as well trained and experienced as we were, and it was a pleasure to train with them. Most people have heard of the rollicking personality of the Scotch and Irish, and this became readily apparent with these guys. They enjoyed joking around and found humor in strange places. Anyone who has spent any time in a hospital has undoubtedly heard announcements over the paging system. At Norfolk General Hospital this system was manned by young women who had no medical training and who simply received a message for someone to be paged and promptly announced the page over the system. The pagee frequently was a physician, and the usual page was "Dr. Smith, Dr. John Smith." Dr. Smith would then call the operator, who would give him the message. Well, medical jargon lends itself to some strange fictitious names if they are split apart and one day we were surprised, but delighted to hear a page for "Dr. Rubin, Dr. Billy Rubin." Now, to the layperson this might not seem strange, except that there was no Dr. Billy Rubin; it was a play on the term, "bilirubin," which is a chemical substance produced in the liver. All of us in the know appreciated the joke and, though we never found out who pulled it, we assumed that it was one of our compatriots from across the pond. After this one sneaked by the page operator, it was not at all unusual to hear other fictional physicians being paged, especially when a new page operator was being broken in or a new crop of interns and residents came in. Some of the "new physicians" were paged as:

Dr. Cardia, Dr. Dexter Cardia (dextrocardia is an anatomic reversal of the heart from the left to the right.)

Dr. Monas, Dr. Sudie Monas (pseudomonas is a bacterial organism)

Dr. Robertson, Dr. Argyll Robertson (Argyll Robertson is the name for a neurological abnormality of the eye, often seen in patients with syphilis.)

Dr. O'Graft, Dr. Al O'Graft (easy to slip by the page operator because of all of the Irish physicians in the hospital, but allograft is the name for a type of tissue transplant.)

Dr. Verdin, Dr. Billy Verdin (biliverdin is also a substance made in the liver.)

Dr. Nevus, Dr. Harry Nevus (a hairy nevus is a dark brown mole with hair growing in it.)

Dr. Robe, Dr. Anna Robe (an anaerobe is a germ that can grow without the presence of oxygen in contrast to an aerobe which requires oxygen to grow.)

Dr. Tall, Dr. Donna Tall (Donnatal is a medicine used to treat stomach disorders.)

Eventually, the administration became aware of the game and educated the page operators on the proper names and gave the page operators a list of approved pagees. However, one additional fictional physician later got paged, much to the chagrin of one of the attending neurosurgeons whose name was subverted, but that is another story.

Sam

During my internship and residency we lived in an apartment building on the campus which was located on the banks of the Elizabeth River. One winter night I was taking our bassett hound, Sam, on his late-night walk. Snow was flying, and a brisk wind was blowing off the river. Since it was late and there was no traffic on this part of the campus, I let Sam off his leash, and he trotted off, happily snuffling the ground and savoring those scents which only such hounds can appreciate. Off to my right I could see a number of vehicles in front of the hospital entrance waiting to pick up nurses getting off the 3:00 P.M. to 11:00 P.M. shift. The wind was to my back, and leaves and pieces of paper occasionally blew by me into the alley between two buildings in front of me. As I sauntered along watching Sam, I spied an insubstantial white something blowing in the wind between the buildings. At first, I thought this was a newspaper or plastic bag being blown along by the wind, but on second glance, the thing remained at the same height and was moving purposefully into the wind toward me. Suddenly curious, I centered all my attention on this apparition, and, as it emerged out of the gloom of the alley, I saw that it was a small black man who was stark naked except for a hospital gown. He had the gown on backward and tied only at the neck which allowed the gown to billow out behind him like Superman's cape. I was later to learn that he had escaped from the psychiatric ward on the fourth floor by jumping out of a window onto the roof of a shorter building below and then making his way down an outside fire escape. At the time, the nursing staff was not even aware of his escape.

About the time I caught sight of the man, Sam also saw him and gave a startled, "whuff," a sound apparently not lost on the man, for he started running pell-mell toward the front of the hospital. Sam, being the hound that he was, and sensing a chase, started off in hot pursuit and in full bay. For those readers who have heard a bassett in full voice, I need say nothing more; for those who haven't, suffice it to say, one would expect to see creature much larger than Sam's already prodigious sixty pounds! At any rate, the man tore across the snow-covered grass, ran through several box bushes and a holly hedge, the latter giving him a few seconds' edge, as Sam had to find a way through the bottom of the hedge. Finally, the man and Sam had a clear shot to the hospital entrance, where a number of nurses were gathered awaiting their rides. As the duo drew closer and the people could see what was happening, many of them made a beeline for the double doors and dashed inside; others who could not get in, sprinted down the sidewalk in the opposite direction. The man turned to see Sam gaining rapidly, and, as he sought refuge from the baying hound, he came abreast of the first car in the line. In a flash, he opened the passenger door and jumped inside, which action resulted in the driver just as rapidly exiting the opposite side and holding the door shut.

Amazingly, all of this took place in less than a minute, and it took me a little longer to reach the scene and corral Sam, who was circling the car and baying at the top of his hound voice. I finally got the leash back on him while the little man sat shivering in the car, and the driver stood outside looking in. In short order, the hospital security guards showed up and were able to coax the man out of the car and back up onto the fourth floor. I decided that we had had enough excitement and exercise for one night, and I walked Sam back to the apartment on his leash with his "tail carried gaily in hound fashion," as described by all of the books on bassett hounds. When we got back to the apartment I told my wife all of what had happened, but she didn't believe a word of it!

In retrospect, the incident probably saved the man's life, as he was confused and would likely have died of exposure before being found. Maybe we should have bestowed an honorary doctorate on Sam!

Allen

Allen Stein's eventual goal was to become an ear-nose-throat surgeon, but his program at Norfolk General Hospital required him to become familiar with the full spectrum of surgery, including general surgery, plastic surgery, neurosurgery, and urology. His first rotation in June 1968 was neurosurgery; his mentor was Dr. McFarthin, a stern and abrupt neurosurgeon who brooked no nonsense. Neurosurgery is, by its nature, an exacting science that allows no margin for error, and Dr. McFarthin was the perfect purveyor of that science. Unfortunately, Allen was not so perfect. If he was to become an excellent otorhinolaryngologist, he was a mediocre neurosurgeon, though he tried hard to get it right.

I was on duty in the emergency room one night when the rescue squad brought in a lovely young woman who had been involved in a motor vehicle accident and who was comatose. Evaluation by the ER staff revealed a skull fracture, and Allen was called to further evaluate the situation. He responded quickly and enthusiastically, eager to make a good impression. He examined the young woman and noted her unresponsiveness. A cursory evaluation of the skull x-rays confirmed the radiologist's hand-written impression of "linear skull fracture." Not having much experience with management of these fractures, but wanting to appear efficient and well prepared for Dr. McFarthin, Allen proceeded to get her ready for brain surgery by cutting off all of her hair. He then meticulously shaved her head, as he told me proudly, without a single nick. He threw the voluminous mass of blond hair in the kick-bucket under the table just as Dr. McFarthin arrived. I was in the next cubicle over from this woman, and was witness to the following events. After a brief consultation in the hallway with Allen, Dr. McFarthin came into the room, and examined the woman from a neurosurgical perspective and looked over the skull x-rays with a practiced eye. He said to Allen, "Well, this young lady has suffered a minor skull fracture with a concussion. She does not need surgery and we will manage her medically. Put her on my service upstairs." Allen looked dumbfounded as Dr. McFarthin started out of the room. And then, struck by sudden realization, Dr. McFarthin stopped short in the doorway, slowly turned around and fixed Allen with a steely eye and asked, "Doctor Stein, where is that woman's hair?" Allen was standing by the kick-bucket and, as if in slow motion, he reached into the bucket and pulled out the mass of soggy hair. Dr. McFarthin looked at the hair, then at the bald woman, back to the hair, and finally at Allen. The silence was deafening! He slowly shook his head and walked off down the hallway muttering something I couldn't hear.

Things did not go well with Allen and Dr. McFarthin for the rest of the rotation. Allen was constantly behind the eight ball, late to rounds, late to surgery, failing to order the proper tests, and omitting a myriad of other small details, which drove Dr. McFarthin to distraction. This tenuous relationship between attending physician and resident became a topic of discussion among the rest of the house staff, and poor Allen got the brunt of a lot of teasing. The final straw as far as Dr. McFarthin was concerned occurred, thankfully, at the end of Allen's rotation, when the page operator was fooled again into a request to page "Dr. McFarstein Dr. Allen McFarstein." I understood later that Dr. McFarthin was furious, and a search for the culprit was undertaken, but no one ever learned the identity of the mad pager.

Allen's next rotation was general surgery, and there was hope that he could salvage some of his reputation as a surgery resident. If he had only known what the near future held, he would probably have folded his tent and stolen away under cover of darkness. Dr. V. was a general surgeon with a reputation as irascible. He was known to reduce house staff to trembling blobs, and Allen was no exception. He was scheduled on an abdominal procedure with Dr. V. and was nervous to begin with. Matters got worse when their case was bumped to a later time due to an emergency appendectomy. When they finally got in the operating room, Dr. V. was obviously angry, and was snapping orders left and right as the patient was prepped and draped for the procedure. To make matters even worse, the air conditioning was not working properly, and the room was uncomfortably warm. Nevertheless, the operation got underway, and Allen was right in the thick of things as the first surgical assistant. Dr. V. was frequently telling him to change this or do that, and Allen was beginning to sweat. Sweating in the operating room is not unusual, and it is customary to ask the float nurse to use a towel to wipe the sweat. Unfortunately, for some reason, Allen did not request a face wipe, and a drop of sweat ran down his nose and fell onto the sterile drapes around the incision. Dr. V. threw down his instruments and bellowed, "Doctor, why don't you just defecate in the wound?" Allen was mortified and staggered back from the table to sit down on a stool promptly supplied by the float nurse. Dr. V. ripped and snorted the entire time the contaminated drapes were removed and new ones put in place.

Eventually, all was ready, and the procedure was resumed. Again, Allen was sweating profusely, but he had the presence of mind to have the float nurse wipe the river flowing off his forehead. Unfortunately, she did not take off his glasses and wipe his nose and the back of his ears and slowly, but inexorably the glasses began to slide down his nose. He tried to hitch them up by wiggling his nose in reverse and flicking his head up in the air. Dr. V. apparently was not aware of the drama being played out and kept snapping at Allen to "hold this retractor, hand me that hemostat, stop shaking," etc, etc. And with the last head shake, the glasses went flying off and landed right in the incision! That was the last straw, and Dr. V. said, in barely controlled fury, "Goddammit, Stone, get the hell out of my operating room!" [Stone was not Allen's last name.]

As Allen walked dejectedly toward the door, Dr. V. added, "And come back and get your damned glasses."

When Allen related this to me later, he said, "But you know the best thing? He doesn't know who I am!"

I lost track of Allen, and I don't know if he ever realized his dream of becoming an ENT surgeon, but one thing is sure, wherever he is, he has some funny stories to tell, but only in retrospect.

Dr. M.

As I progressed through the general part of my training, I functioned as a first-year surgical resident and, as luck would have it, I was helping Dr. M. operate on an indigent patient who had suffered a depressed skull fracture. Unlike simple linear skull fractures, these commonly have to be "elevated" to remove the pressure on the brain. Dr. M., with my help, had completed the procedure without any problems, although in my boredom with suctioning the blood from the field, the suction tip would wander too close to the brain tissue, and Dr. M. would snap, "Don't suck the brain!"

After the procedure we went to check on the patient, who had a room in the old part of the hospital that had been retained even after the new hospital had been built. The two buildings were connected by a long overhead walkway, and I could tell that Dr. M. was in a hurry. The old building had very narrow hallways, and as we neared the patient's room we came up upon a nurse who was trying to maneuver an unwieldy bed into a cross hall by pulling it along behind her. I waited behind Dr. M for several very long seconds as she slowly worked it into the cross hall, and when there was just enough room to get by, Dr. M. squeezed into the slowly widening space, and to give himself more room to get by, he gave the bed a shove. The bed shot forward, hit the nurse right behind the knees, and she fell backwards onto the bed! My last recollection was seeing her upended in the foot of the bed with her feet sticking straight up in the air. Dr. M. marched on down the hall, impervious to the scene he had left behind, and my trying to maintain an air of dignity without bursting into laughter.

My Consultant

The indigent clinic area at Norfolk General Hospital was not designed to be private, but to utilize space most effectively. The rooms were large and partitioned only by cloth drapes drawn between the beds. Usually there was a small desk and a couple of chairs that the physicians could use in talking with patients. Patients, family, and friends sat in the hallways right outside of the exam rooms, and, as routine maintenance took place at the same time we were examining patients, it was not unusual to see workers with their paraphernalia walking up and down the halls. Designers of the modern HIPPA rules would most certainly have had apoplexy at the arrangement. It was in this arrangement that Douglas, one of our OB-GYN residents, was doing a pelvic examination on a woman when he looked up to see a well-dressed man peering around the curtain. The "out of sight" rule having been broken, Doug assumed that this must be the woman's husband and motioned for him to come around to the end of the table where he explained in detail his findings pointing out pertinent anatomical features. The man seemed very interested and made appropriate responses at the right times, and when Doug got up to let the woman dress, the man proceeded into the hall, picked up his bucket and ladder and walked off down the hall. Realizing his mistake, Doug went back to the cubicle after the woman had gotten dressed, sat down at the desk with her, and summarized his findings and his plan of care. He also carefully added that the visiting consultant had agreed fully with his plans!

Eddie

I was fortunate to have not only excellent teachers at Norfolk General Hospital, but excellent co-workers as well. The house staff had been carefully selected and represented the best of their medical-training programs before coming to Norfolk to complete their training. There is little doubt that the physicians in any postgraduate program learn as much from each other as we learn from our teachers. One-up-manship played a big role in our interaction, and we were not shy about flaunting our newfound knowledge; neither were we reluctant to pull a fast one on our fellow house-staff members. As an intern on the medical service, I frequently worked with Eddie Bauman, who was training in internal medicine. Late one night Eddie and I were called to a cardiac arrest. As was my modus operandi, even if I had to race to the scene, I always made sure to walk into the room in complete control so as not to give the nurses the impression that I was flustered. So I sprinted down the hall, took the stairs two at a time, took a shortcut through a classroom, and arrived on the floor in short order. Despite my frantic dash to the floor, I slowed to a sedate walk to the room and strolled in cool and slow to give the impression that I was not ruffled and would soon have everything under control. I found, however, that Eddie had been on the floor and already had everything under control. Unfortunately, our prompt arrival was for naught, and, as we watched, the EKG gradually went flat, and Eddie pronounced the patient deceased. He told me to go to the nurse's station and take care of all of the paperwork (interns always have to do the paperwork) while he completed activities in the room. A few minutes later, one of the nurses came running up to the desk, and told me that Dr. Bauman needed me immediately. I hastened into the room where Eddie was standing next to the bed looking at the EKG. To my astonishment it was running off an entirely normal tracing! My Joe Cool state instantly evaporated as I tried to figure this out. The patient looked no more alive than when I had left the room; there was no respiration, no pulse, and I could not hear a heartbeat. I looked at Eddie, shaking my head in bewilderment, and then it hit me…there were no EKG leads on the patient's chest! As I looked back at Eddie, he grinned and slowly pulled up his smock to show the leads fastened to his own chest! The room erupted in laughter, and I had learned a good lesson, albeit a sneaky one: don't be fooled by discrepancies in observation; there is usually an explanation.

Will and the Heartworms

As the term implies, family physicians care for the age spectrum from the cradle to the grave, so when I was looking for a postgraduate training center, I was interested in the quality of the pediatric training as well as that of the adult population. Norfolk General Hospital was affiliated with the Children's Hospital of the King's Daughters, the only free-standing children's hospital in the state, and the pediatric portion of my training was done in that center. In addition to knowing the reputation of King's Daughters, I knew several of the physicians ahead of me there and knew of their training and expertise and felt comfortable that we would work well together. One of these physicians was Will Gay, who had graduated ahead of me at the University of Virginia. I knew him as a "regular guy" who was renowned at UVa for his prowess at a pool table. Will was a pool shark! I wouldn't say that Will was "hickish," but his appearance and demeanor would not suggest his ability with a pool cue. He won many pool tournaments in Charlottesville and its environs, and many were the self-proclaimed billiard experts who contributed to his spending cash! The wagers were laid out, the balls racked, and the expert watched as Will ran the table, picked up the money, and headed out with his spending cash for the week!

Dr. Jim Stone and I were on pediatrics at the same time, and the three of us were constantly challenging each other with the minutiae of medicine in general and pediatrics in particular. Jim and I could compete in the general-medicine arena, but Will dominated the pediatrics. It was a game with us to see who could "scoop" the others, and one weekend I thought I had found the coup de grâce. Our bassett hound, Sam, had been diagnosed with heartworms, a tiny parasitic worm carried by mosquitoes that infects the blood, and I was curious to see them under a microscope. I drew some blood from Sam and took it to the hospital pathology lab, where I put a drop on a slide and focused it under the microscope. Teeming in the drop of blood were dozens of wriggling heartworms. As I looked at them, a ruse slowly took place in my mind, and I called Will at home to help me solve a pediatric dilemma. I told him of a child who had just arrived in the emergency room with a strange illness consisting of a multitude of disjointed symptoms, none of which suggested any disease I could think of. I told him that I had a blood smear that I thought he would like to see and which might shed light on the etiology of the disease. He arrived shortly, and asked a series of questions to pinpoint the disease, and when he had exhausted his repertoire, he sat down at the microscope and peered at the parasites squirming in the drop of blood. After a minute or so, he said, "You know, this is really amazing. You have probably found the only case in history of a child with canine heartworms! When you publish this case, you'll be famous!" I stood there with my mouth hanging open as he got up from the microscope and left the lab without another word. I was still in shock as I went home and told my wife the story. She looked a little chagrined and then said, "I saw Will as he was leaving the apartment and told him about Sam and the heartworms."

The only saving grace was that at least he had not come up with that on his own.

Mark

Late night was an excellent time to learn, as things in the hospital were slower, and people had more time to interact. Such was the case one winter night when I was on surgical call with the chief surgical resident, Mark Castert. A patient came into the ER with acute appendicitis, and Mark and I were assigned to do the appendectomy. I had been on the surgery service for several months and had gained some proficiency in surgical technique, and Mark asked me if I would like to do the procedure. I jumped at the chance, although with some trepidation, as would be expected with a first-time procedure. I had studied this common operation in the textbooks and had been the first assistant on a number of them, but doing it yourself is a different matter entirely, and I was understandably nervous. As the patient was being prepped and draped, and we were scrubbing, Mark ran through the procedure as well as the anatomy and what we would find when we got to the infected appendix. I was trembling a little when we stepped up to the table, but once I got the scalpel in my hand and made the opening incision, I became much more at ease, and with Mark's guidance, I managed a slow, but fairly good operation. We closed and dressed the incision, and I was feeling quite proud of myself as we took off our gowns, gloves and masks. When we were out in the hall, Mark said, "Well, Booker, as a surgeon, you are really slow, but..." and here I expected to hear something like, "you do pretty good work," but instead, he finished, "you do damned poor work!" Then he laughed and slapped me on the back, and I knew I really had done pretty well for my first time.

Early to Bed

Jim was an OB-GYN resident. One night his wife Betty had invited several couples over for dinner, and afterward we were all sitting around chatting, when Jim got up and, without a word, left the room. We all thought that he had gone to answer the call of nature, but when he did not come back, we asked Betty if he was sick. "Oh, no," she replied nonchalantly, "he's gone to bed. He always goes to bed at 10:00. I thought everyone knew that." Well, we didn't know, but, in retrospect, it certainly seemed reasonable, given the unpredictability of his schedule as an obstetrician and his need for sleep when he could get it.

Under the Gurney!

The emergency room can be a wild and dangerous place, not only for patients, but for physicians and nurses as well. One night Charlie and I were working as interns in the ER at Norfolk General Hospital when a woman was brought in after she and her boyfriend had gotten into an argument, and he wound up cutting her with a knife. The room had two sections, and I was already working on a patient in the section next to the door, so this woman was put in the next section, and Charlie was called to suture the cuts. He was busy sewing when there was a commotion out in the hall, and suddenly there appeared in the doorway, a man who, though inebriated, was obviously the boyfriend, and the boyfriend had a gun. He spied the woman on the Gurney, pointed the gun at Charlie, and said, "If I can't have her, nobody's gonna have her!"

Charlie turned pale and sweaty, and while getting up from the stool said, "Hey, man, I don't want her, I'm just sewing her up."

The boyfriend replied, "If you sew her up, she'll live and go out with somebody else."

Well, as the discussion went on, Charlie got up and eased to the toilet at the end of the room, slowly turned the doorknob and with a mad lunge slammed into the door, only to find that the door was locked from the other side! From the recoil off the door, Charlie bounced onto the floor and scooted under Gurney as the man cocked the gun and took aim. At that fortuitous moment, the security guard arrived and knocked the gun from the man's hand and wrestled him to the floor. From there the police then took him off to jail.

Later the incident provided a degree of levity as Charlie, who was African-American, said "I didn't turn white, but I was a terrible shade of pale."

The Air Force Years

The Berry Plan

As mentioned previously, my three-year training at Norfolk General Hospital was interrupted by my stint in the United States Air Force from July 1970 to June 1972. The details of how this came about give some insight into the military medical culture during that critical time in our country. In the late 1960s and early 1970s, we were still embroiled in the Vietnam War, and because of the need for general medical officers (GMOs) in the military, physicians were liable to be drafted at anytime regardless of where they were in their medical training. This wreaked havoc with our training and completely disrupted the continuity of specialist training programs around the country. It also did not serve the military very well, as they could not be guaranteed of having adequate numbers of specialists, since they were drafting physicians before they completed their training. The solution came in the form of the Berry Plan. The plan was basically a military deferment lottery system consisting of two parts that each participating physician elected. The first was the branch of the service desired, and the second was the length of deferment. For example, a physician eligible for military service first signed up with the plan. He or she then chose which military branch was desired, Army, Navy or Air Force, and then chose the length of time desired to complete the training program. These were thrown into the lottery, and the names drawn out one by one with the physicians allotted to a service and then given the length of deferment, varying from one or two years to however many years it took to complete the training program. After completion of the Berry Plan program, the physician was obligated to complete his or her military service.

This plan had something for everyone: the physicians knew which service they were going to and how long they had before having to go into the service, the training programs knew how long their trainees would be available, and the military knew how many physicians and what specialists they would be getting each year. Of course, those physicians who did not sign up for the Berry Plan were fair game for drafting at anytime, and the military could snatch them up at any point in their training and make them GMOs. Most of us felt a little more secure knowing what the future held, and the majority of us elected the plan. I was fortunate to be chosen for the Air Force and a full deferment for completing my training at Norfolk General Hospital. At it turned out, I elected to complete two years of training, went in the Air Force for two years, and then completed the last year of my residency in family medicine after getting out of the service.

As the second year of my deferment came to a close, and I had to make plans for entering the Air Force, Norfolk General Hospital hired a new medical director who was a retired Army colonel. Colonel Dr. Raymond Maret had been all over the world in the Army Medical Corps and had connections reaching deeply into all service branches. When I went to talk to him about my options, he told me about his work in Alaska doing research on man's ability to conduct warfare in frigid environments. The more he talked, the more interested I became, and I asked him if he could get me an assignment in Alaska. It was not six hours later that he called me to say that I would be going to the 5074th United States Air Force medical facility in Kenai, Alaska, which was known as Wildwood Air Force Station. Not only that, but because of my two years of training in general medicine and being a captain, I would be the highest-ranking medical officer, and hence the commander of the facility! My years in Alaska would be some of the most interesting years of my medical career.

Shepard Air Force Base

Before I took up my post in Kenai, I had to spend two weeks at Shepard Air Force Base in Wichita Falls, Texas, for basic training. My wife and I had bought a sixteen-foot travel trailer and a new Chevrolet Blazer that we took to and from and all over Alaska in our spare time, but our first major outing was two miserably hot weeks in the Red River Valley. I was mostly inside during the day for training sessions and, since the trailer was not air conditioned, my wife, Mimi, and our young daughter, Margaret, spent most of the days in the campground's little office in front of the air conditioner. It was doubly miserable for Mimi, as she was five months pregnant with our second child, Jake. Thank goodness it cooled off at night and became a little more bearable.

Shepard was the training center for physicians, dentists, and lawyers, and we were told at the beginning of our training that, despite our professional status, we would be taught the basics of marching in formation. The only reprieve would be if the temperature at noon exceeded 103 degrees. We never marched! We joked that a sneaky lawyer managed to get a match under the thermometer right before it was read each day; if so, it would have been the only good thing they did.

It seemed that one or another lawyer took exception to everything that went on, and they complained ad infinitum. The saving grace came one afternoon when General Jerome Wheeler gave a masterful lecture on the development of American foreign policy since World War I. When he finished, one condescending lawyer, an evidently self-styled expert on American foreign policy, took issue with General Wheeler on the impact of the Monroe Doctrine. He asked a very detailed question which lost most of us in its convolutions, and we were starting to feel bad for General Wheeler in face of this thinly veiled and seemingly erudite attack. We needn't have worried. After the questioner had sat down, General Wheeler proceeded to take the guy apart point by point, argument by argument, and limb by limb until there was nothing left to say! As one, all of the physicians and dentists rose and gave him a standing ovation!

On to Anchorage

From Shepard, we drove up east of the continental divide, crossed over the Rockies into western Canada and then to Prince Rupert, where we boarded a ferry that took us up the inside passage to Haines, Alaska. From there we drove to Elmendorf Air Force Base in Anchorage, where I was indoctrinated in the ways of the Arctic. One of the first things we were taught was the "thirty-thirty-thirty rule" of the north; at thirty degrees below zero in a thirty mile-an-hour wind, exposed flesh freezes solid in thirty seconds! That made an impression on me, as did the lecture on earthquakes, when all of a sudden the hanging fluorescent lights began to sway, the windows began to rattle, and the doors began to swing slowly on their hinges. The fellow sitting next to me suddenly sprang out of his seat and dived under the lecturer's table. After the tremors stopped, he sheepishly crawled out from under the table and in a quaking voice told us he had been in Anchorage during the 1964 earthquake that devastated the area! After visiting Earthquake Park later that week and then seeing the eight-foot drop of the land along Turnagain Arm as a result of the quake and the subsequent tsunami, I could appreciate his reaction.

And Thence to Wildwood

After finishing my cold-weather indoctrination, we headed south to the Wildwood 5074th USAF base, where we were housed in a two-story duplex apartment. The base was used for satellite downloads, and all other functions on the base were in support of that goal. The dispensary was primarily an outpatient facility, but we did have a ward room and one private room for hospitalizing acutely ill patients. We had laboratory and x-ray facilities and a fully equipped operating room, the rationale for the latter being it was safer to fly in a surgeon from Elmendorf than to try to transport an acutely ill surgical patient to

Anchorage, especially in bad weather. We also used the operating room to deliver babies if we did not have time or the ability to get the mother to the hospital at Elmendorf. Interestingly, the physicians at Wildwood before our staff came, were leery of the prospect of delivering babies there, and they routinely sent the pregnant women to Elmendorf a week before their due date. This, obviously, resulted in some women staying in the delivery suite at Elmendorf for an extended length of time, which was considered "ineffective use of resources." I was told that since we were not specifically trained in obstetrics, they wanted us to send the expectant mothers to Elmendorf for delivery, but "only a few days before they go into labor!" We really never figured out how to do that, so we delivered a few babies right there on base.

Nyle Lower, NCOIC

Our staff at Wildwood consisted of two physicians, Dr. B. and I, two female nurses, a dentist, a dental hygienist, a lab tech, an x-ray tech, several support corpsmen, and a facility manager, who was an inactive paratrooper-medic named Nyle Lower, who was the non-commissioned officer in charge of the clinic. One morning I got to the clinic to find it in chaos due to some scheduling mistakes and the sickness of several of the staff. As I was trying to get things straightened out, Nyle came bustling through the back door, sized up the situation and told me, "Captain, what you need here is someone with a little authority, and I'm just your man; I have about as little authority as anyone!" He then proceeded in the next five minutes to get everything humming again!

Nyle is also the subject of another humorous event on base. Winter in Alaska is a snowy affair, and unlike the more moderate climes, which allow snow to melt between storms, snow in Alaska does not melt. Removal is therefore problematic; it can't be just pushed out of the way with snow plows, it has to be blown up and over the previous piles. This results in some unbelievable banks of snow, and this was the case around our helicopter landing pad, which we used frequently because we had no landing strip. The first winter we were there was especially snowy, and the banks around the pad were probably ten to fifteen feet tall, causing the pad to look like a big room without a ceiling. It was into this room that we had to call the big Huey helicopter to evacuate a pregnant woman one night. We had never had to do this at night and, as usual, we turned to Nyle for the proper protocol. He said that it was no big deal; all we had to do was have someone direct the helicopter down using those long-snouted red flashlights like they use on aircraft carriers to direct planes onto and off the flight deck. We just happened to have a set of them, and Nyle just happened to know how to use them, so our anxiety level was much diminished. We got into our arctic gear, bundled the patient in warm blankets on the stretcher and went with Nyle who was wearing a neon-orange flight suit and carrying the flashlights. We positioned ourselves at the edge of the pad while Nyle stood in the center-front of the pad so that the pilot could see his hand signals. As the helicopter came over the tree line, I was amazed at the size of the thing, never having seen one up close before. It came right over the pad with Nyle's signals and began to settle onto the pad. Then the unexpected happened. The air-wash from the blades was tremendous, and as it hit the pad and blasted outward, it picked up Nyle and flung him right into the bank of snow. With snow flying wildly, it was not until the pilot shut down the rotors that we could even see where he went, and then we had to search for a few seconds until someone spotted one neon orange leg sticking out of the bank. The laboring woman on the stretcher was forgotten for a few minutes as we dug Nyle out of the bank. We made sure he was all right, and we then returned to where she was waiting, to find her laughing so hard we were afraid she would deliver right there. Fortunately, all turned out well. Nyle was injured only insofar as his pride was wounded, and the woman made it to Elmendorf and delivered without any problems. All's well that ends well.

Those Fingers

Dr. B. was the other physician on the base, and he and I got along well. He had been trained at Wilford Hall Medical Center, the Air Force's physician training center, and he was an excellent general physician. He had lost the ends of his right fore and middle fingers in a wood shop accident in high school, but this in no way detracted from his surgical skills, and he enjoyed doing the procedures we were capable of doing there. One afternoon he had an appointment with an airman and his wife to discuss doing a vasectomy. He went over the procedure in detail and told the airman to make an appointment when he wanted to have it done. As they left to consider the procedure, I overheard the wife say "Listen, Patrick, before you let him do that operation, you'd better find out how he lost those fingers!"

A Bad Accident

Christmas Eve the first year I was at Wildwood was a cold and stormy night with high winds and heavy snow. Dr. B. was on call, and about 10:30 that night he called, and in an excited voice, said, "We've had a bad accident, and this fellow is really in bad shape. I think he's going to need an operation." My heart came up in my throat, as I knew there was no way by air, land, or sea that anything was going to move on this night! Whatever had to be done, we were going to have to do it. With fear and trepidation, I ran over to the clinic to find Dr. B. in the operating room with our badly injured "patient," a small white poodle that had apparently been hit by a snowmobile. The poodle belonged to a base family that had several children who were devastated by the injury and the knowledge that their father had brought the dog to us to be put to sleep. Dr. B was also upset, primarily because it was Christmas Eve, and this poodle was the children's special pet. He said, "Do you think we can operate on this little guy and save him?" Fortunately, I had done a number of surgical procedures during my summer with our hometown vet and also in the dog lab at the University of Virginia. In fact, I had actually done a splenectomy, which we wound up having to do on the poodle. Dr. B wanted to do the procedure, so I put the dog to sleep with mask ether and then assisted Dr. B in cleaning up the wound, repairing several bowel perforations, and taking out the spleen, which was badly lacerated and would not stop bleeding. We repaired the peritoneum and closed the wound as best we could. We then put the little fellow in our private room where we could keep track of him better and started him on our outdated penicillin and streptomycin. Amazingly, he did not die that night, or the next or the next, and then began to eat and then to run around and eventually to recover completely except for some fecal incontinence at times, which the family did not mind at all. All in all, an amazing tale, considering our lack of sophisticated surgical training.

But that is not the end of the story. On the 27th the weather still had not cleared, and we got a message from the local rescue squad that a retired army colonel living in Soldotna, just up the road from Kenai, had become ill and had to have medical attention. Since our facility served all military branches, we asked if they could get him in to us. They arranged for a snow blower to get to the colonel's house with the rescue squad following in their four-wheel-drive ambulance. They then followed the snow blower to our clinic. The colonel was quite ill with pneumonia, and we recommended that he stay in the clinic until we could get the infection under control with IV antibiotics. Our nurses arranged to cover the nights with him, the corpsmen helped out during the daytime, and we succeeded in getting him back on his feet in a few days. The problem was the dog in the private room! The colonel was certainly not cramped in the ward room, as he was the only patient (human) we had at the time, but we were a little worried about what he might think about sharing a medical facility with a dog. Accordingly, all of us worked diligently to keep the colonel happy and the dog quiet while we healed both of them. The dog was a quiet little fellow and made no fuss at all, and we kept the door closed all the time. The staff was in and out all during the day, and we felt we had done a good job in our clandestine venture. The colonel improved rapidly, and on the 31st we bade him farewell, a much happier man than when he had come in. As Dr. B. and I got him into his car and shook his hand, he said, "Thanks for everything, and I sure hope the dog gets along all right." So much for clandestine!

It Takes a Big Dog

Every Monday morning all of the divisions on the base had a staff meeting with the base commander, Colonel Kitts. He conducted a very democratic meeting and always asked at the end if anyone had any other business to discuss. On one Monday, he ended up by asking if anyone had anything to say. He seemed a little put out that no one responded, as though we were covering up some vital information. He was quiet for a few moments, and then asked Captain Joe McCleland if he did not have something he wanted to say. Joe sat there blank-faced, but feeling he had to say something; his response astounded us all when he said, "Well, Colonel Kitts, it takes a big dog to weigh 500 pounds!" We sat there with held breaths fully expecting fire and brimstone from the commander who just stood there speechless. After an eternity, he burst out laughing and, dismissed us all with a salute!

Worms

Winter in Alaska can be long and dreary, and we and our fellow officers sought multiple ways of alleviating the boredom. One Saturday night Mimi and I had been invited, along with several other couples, to Bill's and Dawn's apartment for dinner. Dawn had planned a very fashionable dinner complete with an appetizer of escargot, which she had managed to get from the base commissary. We all had children, and they were included in the invitation. Since Margaret was about three years old at the time, Dawn seated her at the table across from Joe McCleland of the above story. As Dawn put the escargot on the table, and while we were all gnawing away on the tough little critters, Mimi convinced Margaret to try one. She reluctantly put one in her mouth which she chewed and chewed and rolled it around, finally spitting it out on the table with the exclamation, "Worm!" Joe almost choked on his and after recovering, said, "My sentiments exactly, Margaret" whereby, we all agreed that Dawn had done all she could do to present the things in an attractive way, but there is just so much you can do to a snail!

Flying

With two physicians on our small base, each of us had a fair amount of free time. Dr. B. had learned to fly light planes when he was in Texas and bought a Cessna 170 in Alaska. His tales of flying struck a chord with me, and I enrolled in a flying course offered by the University of Alaska and then began taking lessons. My instructor was Ray Simmons, who had flown in Viet Nam before coming to Kenai. He was an excellent instructor, but he cut me no slack regarding my initial anxiety about flying. "Relax," he would say. "Don't grip the wheel so tight; sit back and relax." "Don't press the rudder pedals so hard," etc, etc. One day when we were ready to take off, he called the flight tower and announced, "Kenai tower, this is Charlie one-niner-one otherwise known as the 'White Knuckles Airline,' requesting permission for take off on runway 27." In spite of becoming more comfortable with piloting an aircraft and losing the white knuckles, I never lost the moniker.

The owner of the local flight service was an old Air Force mechanic who enjoyed working on the planes but eschewed flying himself. I finally advanced far enough that Ray cut me loose, and I began flying by myself. Whenever I returned from a solo flight, the owner would regard me with a make-believe astonished look and say, "Well, Captain, I see you defied death again!"

Homeward Bound

With Richard Nixon's military cutbacks and the ending of the Viet Nam war, the Wildwood base was closed, and Mimi, the children, and

I headed back to Norfolk to complete the last year of my training. It was an uneventful trip across Canada until we got to Ontario, where we planned to cross over into the United States. As I drew up to the customs booth, I handed over all of our transportation documents allowing us to drive from Alaska through Canada. I had a rifle, a shotgun and a pistol that I had acquired in Alaska and was taking home, and I dutifully handed over the form which I had completed in British Columbia allowing me to transport such dangerous items. The customs official looked at me in horror. He immediately turned and went into the customs booth, where he and several other officials examined the documents. Eventually they all came out and surrounded the car and camper looking us up and down very suspiciously. I was totally confused until the head man walked over to me and showed me the small print, "firearms of any kind may not be transported from the western provinces any further east than Manitoba without legal consequences." My mouth went suddenly dry, and my stomach was in a knot; I had not realized this restriction, and here I was in Ontario, surrounded by customs officials who looked as though they thought I may have committed murder and mayhem on my way across Canada. I freely confessed that I had not known about the regulations and explained how we came to be there, and after several whispered conversations among themselves, the headman pulled me aside and said, "By law we are supposed to report this infraction, but seeing you with your wife, children, a basset hound and a hamster, we cannot possibly suspect you of nefarious intentions, so get in the car and get across the border as fast as you can. And don't look back!"

I took his advice and we proceeded with all haste to Norfolk and the last year of my training before becoming a private physician.

Family Physicians

My second year of residency in Norfolk passed quickly and uneventfully, and during the fall of 1972, Dr. Jim Stone and I agreed to seek a situation where we could practice together. We felt that a rural area would best suit our training, inclination, and capabilities and looked extensively throughout southwestern Virginia. After visiting and evaluating about eight locations, we decided to join Dr. Walter Barton in forming Family Physicians of Wytheville in July of 1973. We operated as a private practice until 1995, when we joined the Carilion Healthcare System headquartered in Roanoke, Virginia, and became known as Carilion Family Physicians of Wytheville, to which I still belong today. During our private-practice years we started out in a small building owned by our senior partner, but later we built a larger office just down the road from the Wythe County Community Hospital. In 1980 we took in another partner, Dr. Wayne Horney, who was raised in Wythe County and who returned to practice here. Over the years we have employed other physicians who, for one reason or another, chose to move on to other practices, as did Dr. Horney in 2007. We lost Dr. Barton to retirement in 1996, and so Jim Stone and I continue as the dinosaurs of the practice, but with two young men, Dr. William Tomiak and Dr. Richard Grube, and one young woman, Dr. Kari Lucas, shoring up the practice, hopefully for a long time. Maybe some day one of these will publish an addendum to these stories of Wytheville and its environs, adding their own version of humor in the medical world.

The tales from this point are all from my years in Wytheville. Most of the stories could have been placed in any of several categories, but

I have attempted to group them in sections that have some cohesiveness and to give some separation instead of a lengthy recitation of story after story. The chapters can be read in any order, but most sense can be made by progressing from front to back, as some of the material depends on the foregoing to be fully understood.

Edna

One of the most delightful women I have met along life's road is Edna Williams Parks, who is not only a dear friend, but worked for us for years as we traversed the path from our private practice to our association with Carilion. Edna is an "old school" girl who has been steeped in the old-fashioned way of doing things. Turpentine cures everything that can be cured, and she can butcher a hog with the best of them. You will meet her again in the "LeRoy Tales," but this next story is about Edna herself and will give you a glimpse into her personality.

Edna came to work one day all dressed up to go to the visitation of Mrs. Smith who had died several days back. We teased her about her mode of dress, which was distinctly out of character for this country girl, but more so because the visitation was not until the next night. She was ruffled, to say the least, and called the funeral home to be sure we were not pulling her leg. The funeral home receptionist confirmed that, indeed, the visitation was the following night. In a great huff, Edna said, "Well, I'm all dressed up to come to a visitation, and I hate to waste it; who you got down there for tonight?"

Republican vs. Democrat

Bob was a dyed-in-the-wool Democrat who enjoyed crossing horns with anyone of contrary persuasion. He had chronic lung disease, and I saw him frequently for bronchitis and occasionally for pneumonia. On one visit he was especially ill and asked me if he was going to die. I told him that despite his feeling so bad, I did not think that he was in any immediate danger of dying. He lightened up quite a bit at that news and then said, "Doctor, I would appreciate it if you could give me about two weeks notification of my kicking the bucket."

"Why on earth do you need to know that, Bob?" I asked.

"Well, I need time to get down to the courthouse to change my registration from Democrat to Republican."

"Why would you want to do that?" I asked.

"Well," he replied, "if somebody's got to die, I want it to be one of them!"

I am pretty sure that Bob never changed his registration. He lived and died a Democrat, and the Republicans were not able to enjoy his company, even for two weeks.

Poison Ivy

Football is big business in Wythe County, and nowhere more than at George Wythe High School here in Wytheville. The training of young football players starts early and progresses right on through high school. George Wythe has won one state championship and come in second in the state another time. The county has seen a number of its football players go on to play in the college ranks. The success of these young men is a tribute to the avid fans who have contributed so much time and money to the cause and to the dedicated coaches who insist on such conditioning as to get the players through the fourth quarter as fresh as in the first. The practice field at George Wythe is long and narrow and is surrounded by a chain link fence, which has seen brush and weeds spring up outside it. In 1991, Coach Mark Robertson was supervising conditioning exercises on this field by running the team from one end of the field to the other several times. To insure that everyone was completing the requisite "to the fence and back" he had each player pick a leaf off the fence and bring it back to prove his fidelity. Such fidelity resulted in most of the players coming down with major cases of poison ivy!

Everybody Is a Doctor

Joann has been under my care for years, but only sporadically. She rarely comes for preventive care, showing up only when she has some condition that reminds her of the reality of the grim reaper. This was the case one morning when she called Robin and stated that she needed to be seen because of the pain in her leg. Although the pain had been present for a week, she had not become concerned until her husband returned from his weekly breakfast with some cronies at a local restaurant. When he mentioned to this group, which included a lawyer or two, about Joann's infirmity, the consensus of opinion was that this was serious business! It might be a blood clot! It could break loose and go to the lungs! It could be fatal! And so on. So when he got home there was no doubt that Joann had to see me posthaste.

She arrived shortly, and subsequent examination revealed no serious condition, although there was certainly a lot of anxiety. I suggested to her that earlier medical intervention would have served two goals: less anxiety and a shorter course of disease. I also told her that any non-legal advice from a lawyer should be taken with a grain of salt, and any medical advice should not be taken at all, since the lawyer then belonged in that large group where "everybody is a doctor." To make the point, I told her the following story.

Dr. Smith passed away and ascended into heaven, where he found a long line of people waiting to have St. Peter check them through the pearly gates. He walked right up to the front of the line and announced to St. Peter that he had just arrived and that his good works on earth should qualify him for immediate admission without having to wait in line. St. Peter told him that in heaven, everyone is equal and that he had to get back in line. Shortly thereafter, Dr. Smith happened to see a young doctor dressed in a white coat, a stethoscope around his neck and a little black bag in hand just walk right through the gates without so much as a glance from St. Peter. Dr. Smith indignantly confronted St. Peter about this saying, "Look here, I've been down there practicing medicine for fifty years, treating the injured, curing the sick, and comforting the bereaved, and you make me wait in line and then you let that young whippersnapper just walk right in. Who was he anyway?" to which St. Peter replied, "Oh, that's God; he likes to play doctor now and then!"

I'm was not sure the story made any impression on Joann, but on her next visit (at which time she was feeling much better), she laughingly related to me that she was not going to "play doctor anymore," but suggested to me that the story could also be taken to imply that doctors sometime play God! I decided that I had better be careful which stories I told and to whom!

Holly

Dr. Holly Smith was the first female primary care physician in Wythe County, and it took some folks a long time to get used to the idea of female physicians. She has practiced in Rural Retreat, Virginia, for years and is much loved by her patients for her thorough and thoughtful manner of care. Early in her career she was on call for unassigned patients, those who have no local physician and are cared for by our physicians on a rotating basis. Dr. Fred Moses was on call in the emergency room when an elderly lady came in with pneumonia and needed to be admitted. Dr. Moses called Holly to take care of her, and in her usual efficient manner, Holly got her well in short order. On the last day of her stay, the lady thanked Holly profusely and then said, "Honey, you've taken real good care of me and I'm feeling great, but when am I going to see the doctor again?"

Miss Imma

Miss Imma was in her mid 80s and had begun to develop Alzheimer's-type dementia. Her mental function tended to fluctuate; at times she was very lucid and other times not so lucid. It was during one of the latter times that her daughter planned to take her shopping. Knowing that her mother frequently needed prodding and reminding, Lydia called several times and was assured that all was going well, and

Imma would be ready on time. On the last call, Imma said rather irritably, "I'm all ready. I am just now combing my hair; come on and get me." When Lydia got there, Imma had indeed gotten her hair combed and put up beautifully and was standing there in nothing but her panties and bra!

Snow and Fire

Dr. Jim Stone had cared for an elderly couple for years and was saddened to hear that the husband had passed away. His wife was in her mid eighties, and sometime later came to the office for a check-up and refill on her medicines. Her husband had always taken care of her medicines, and she was unaware of the details, but she gave Jim a slip of pharmacy logo paper with two numbers on it. She said that she had found this in his wallet and assumed that it would be the correct pharmacy. Jim asked his nurse to call the numbers, and find out if one was, indeed, the correct pharmacy. The first number turned out to be the husband's credit-card number, not a phone number, so she called the second number. Imagine her surprise when she heard a sultry, sexy female voice say, "Hello, sweetheart, are you horney? Just enter your credit card number!"

Jim never told the lady that her husband may have had snow on the roof, but he definitely had a fire in the old furnace!

Optimism

Mr. Grubb was 94 years old and had some walnut trees in his yard that needed to be cut down. He was a woodworker and wanted to save the trees because he wanted to make a bedroom suite out of the wood. He had the logs cut into rough lumber at a local saw mill, and once he got it home, he had it stacked, alternating the boards so that air could circulate between them. He told his son that he wanted the boards to air dry for a few years before he started making the furniture.

What Buggy?

Harvey wasn't anything if not a cut-up. He was from Florida but spent the summers in the cool air of the southwest Virginia mountains. On one of his visits to see me, he told me that he and a friend were out riding one day when they ran across an Amish family driving a horse and buggy down Route 19 in Florida. This was a totally unexpected sight, and his friend was really excited, as he knew of no Amish families in the area. When they got back to their retirement center, his friend began to tell everyone what he had seen. The folks at the home listened politely, but with obvious disbelief. The more he talked about what he had seen, the more people seemed to question his veracity. Finally, in desperation, he turned to Harvey and said, "Tell them, Harvey, we really did see a buggy, didn't we?"

Harvey shrugged his shoulders and said, "What buggy?"

Second-Class Diabetic

This next tale comes to me from my son, Jake, who is now a gynecologist in Florida, but who went to the Medical College of Virginia for his medical school training. An internal medicine resident working in the clinic at MCV had seen a woman with type II, adult-onset diabetes. Because she was a new patient the resident spent a great deal of time with her explaining that weight loss, diet, exercise, and oral medicines would probably take care of the problem. He arranged for her to get more intensive diabetic training and dietary instruction, and felt really good about his handling of the case. He was, then, totally surprised when he was called to a meeting with his attending physician, a patient advocate, and the patient herself to air a complaint that she brought against him. As it turned out, the patient was upset because the resident had called her a "second-class diabetic who didn't deserve insulin!" The case was resolved to everyone's satisfaction.

Leave the Preaching to Me

Mr. Smith was a fundamentalist preacher from Tennessee who, in his later years, made his home in Wythe County. Despite being in his eighties, he remained very active, especially on the revival circuit. On one occasion he had been seeing me for a bout of pneumonia and was recovering very slowly, because he would not slow down and was continuing his ministerial duties. In the office I explained to him that he needed to "cool his heels" and allow himself time to heal. He replied, "Doctor, I'm from Tennessee, and I don't understand these North Carolina terms." I could see that I was not making much headway in convincing him to slow down, so I tried another tactic. I explained that pneumonia is a serious disease, especially in the elderly, and that the slow resolution of these symptoms was probably a sign that he should take it easy. Then, I launched into some Biblical history to make my point and mentioned how Nebuchadnezzar had seen the handwriting on the wall, which was a sign unto him. I said, "You remember the story don't you, Reverend? Old Neb probably had pneumonia and was raring to go back to his kingly duties too soon. As he was getting ready to go out, he saw the handwriting on the wall that said, 'Neb, you've had a bad time of it, old son, now just cool your heels until you get better.'"

Mr. Smith grinned and said, "Son, I like your doctoring, but you'd better leave the preaching to me!"

Harry Is Gone

Hal Pope is a retired science teacher and has been a patient of mine for many years. His father was an old country doctor in the southern part of Wythe County and did obstetrical care as a routine part of his practice. One day Hal had just come out of the grocery store when he was approached by an elderly lady who asked him if he were Dr. Pope's son. Hal told her that he was, and she proceeded to tell him that she had been a patient of his father's and that he had delivered three of her children at home. She related how comforting it was that he would be right in the room sitting on the bed with her. He would read, drink coffee, and smoke cigarettes until the time of delivery, after which he would leave, or if it were late, just spend the night. She said that when she heard that Dr. Pope had died, she told her husband, "We're not sleeping together anymore; Harry Pope is gone."

The Survey

Patient satisfaction is an important factor in modern-day medicine. It no longer suffices simply to "cure the patient;" it is incumbent on the physician to address the feelings of the patient as well. There are many physicians from which to choose, and the business of medicine dictates that we appeal to the patient's sense of satisfaction with his or her entire physician encounter. In that regard we have a system of patient satisfaction surveys to help us judge which areas of the encounter we need to improve. One man's response to his visit with one of my partners stands out as particularly humorous. The specific items were:

What is your health status?
That's what I came here to find out.
Was your privacy respected?
Yes. I was in the room for thirty minutes and nobody bothered me.
What did your doctor do for you?
He got on my last nerve.
Would you recommend this physician to other people?
Yes. To my mother-in-law.
And a backhanded compliment to me came from a patient who had seen one of my partners, and who obviously was not pleased with the encounter.
Other comments?
Thank God for Dr. Booker!

LeRoy Umbarger Tales

LeRoy Umbarger was an old-fashioned man. He was a farmer and a saw miller who lived in a remote section of Bland County in the mountains of southwest Virginia. He was tall, lean, lanky, and the epitome of grizzled. His acquaintance with the razor was casual, and his trips to the barber were infrequent. As befitting his occupations, his attire du jour was usually a flannel shirt, overalls (pronounced "overhauls") and "clodhoppers" (heavy leather, thick-soled, half-boot, lace-up footwear).

I can never remember hearing LeRoy laugh; the closest he got to mirth was a wry grin and a twinkle in his eye. He would never have won any accolades on the comic hour, but LeRoy Umbarger was one of the most humorous men I have ever met. He saw humor in the mundane, and his droll recitations proved endlessly entertaining to his family and friends. I consider myself fortunate to have been counted among his friends.

I'm a Poor Man

It was late one winter afternoon when our receptionist, Edna Williams, came back to my office a little before closing and said that an old farmer had just come in from over in Bland and looked pretty sick. She also noted that he was "a little muddy." I had my nurse bring LeRoy to the examining room and watched as he laid down a trail of dirt clods and mud through the hallway. His "clodhoppers" were well named! Since this was my first encounter with LeRoy, I spent extra time with him, extending well past closing. As would be the case over many years, LeRoy had bronchitis. I wound up giving him an injection of an antibiotic, putting him on several new medicines, and instructing him in the care of his chronic illnesses. Clumping back down the hallway, he added a few more clods to the existing collection. He did not seem to recognize the mess, but if he did, he was unapologetic. I lingered in the hallway as Edna checked over the bill and told Leroy what he owed.

"That will be $6.00, Mr. Umbarger." A short pause.

"What?" He exclaimed, rather loudly.

"$6.00. $4.00 for the office call, $1.00 for being a new patient, and $1.00 for the shot."

"That's a lot of money for a poor man to pay!"

"Well, the doctor did spend a lot of time with you, and after hours, too. And you also got a shot. Doesn't seem like a lot to me."

"I don't have much money with me. How about $4.50, and I'll agree to come back again sometime."

"Well, that's mighty nice of you, but our fee schedule is very reasonable, and I'll have to ask you to pay the $6.00."

"Ma'am, I'm just a poor farmer. I work hard for my money, and it ain't like I wanted to bother you. I just got sick all of a sudden."

"I certainly understand that, Mr. Umbarger, but we have to be paid to keep the office running. And $6.00 is not a lot to pay for the doctor making you well."

"Well, you know the price of food today, and a body's got to eat. I can either pay you or buy food, and here you are trying to separate me from my victuals."

At that point, I was ready to intercede, and write off the visit to goodwill, when "poor LeRoy" reached inside his overalls and pulled out a wad of bills that would have choked a mule, peeled off a ten dollar bill, and, with his wry grin, said, "keep the change."

He had thoroughly enjoyed the interchange.

Come Here Dog

LeRoy's association with "John Rolfe's weed" had rendered him afflicted with chronic lung disease and vascular disease, with resultant slow healing of wounds, especially those on the legs. One day he appeared in my office complaining of a non-healing sore on the right leg, occasioned by being hit by a chunk of wood he had been trying to split with an axe. On examination, there was a quarter-sized raw area on the inside of his right lower leg surrounded by three or four puncture wounds. I probed it a bit, and he jerked back saying, "I've got a little feeling, if you care to know."

I apologized and then said "LeRoy, I understand the ulcer, but what on earth are those other marks?" He looked a little abashed, but related the following tale.

He had become concerned about the long duration of the sore when one day he was sitting on the porch with his old hound dog when he recalled how the "good book" talked about the dogs licking the wounds of Lazarus. Confounding the story to some extent, he concluded that if the dog would lick the wound, perhaps it would heal. He therefore bared his leg and stuck it in front of the dog. Unfortunately, the dog was not interested in licking a purulent, several-weeks-old sore ,so Leroy went in the kitchen and smeared some butter around the sore. The dog once again spurned his advances, and LeRoy went back to the kitchen and sprinkled some sugar in the butter. Presenting his leg to the dog resulted in the same rejection, and LeRoy was getting frustrated. He once again went into the kitchen where his wife had been frying bacon. He got some bacon grease and added that to the existing concoction. Again, he went back on the porch and presented the leg to the dog, and this time, "Damned if he didn't bite me!"

After a course of topical treatment and oral antibiotics, the wound finally healed without untoward complications.

A Pinned-up Shirttail

Antibiotics are double-edged swords. They can cure bacterial infections, but are associated with a number of side effects, one of which is diarrhea. Usually this is self-limited, but can be bothersome at times. LeRoy had been to see me for a bout of pneumonia, and I had given him an antibiotic. On his next visit to me I asked him how he got along with the treatment. He said, "Well, doctor, the pneumonia did okay, but I had to pin my shirttail up for about a week." I gathered that his trips to the toilet were numerous and precipitate.

In Retrospect

Boars are a necessity if one is to successfully raise hogs, and the acquisition of a new boar hog is reason for visitation and celebration. LeRoy's neighbor up the road had just bought a dandy new boar and invited LeRoy to come up early one morning to see the new fellow. As they walked down to the hog pen, the neighbor stopped by an outhouse and pulled a board loose, reached into the revealed space and extracted "a mason jar." At this point, LeRoy favored me with his trademark grin and a wink, subtly letting me know that "the mason jar" contained something other than spring water. They went on down to the hog pen, and each propped a foot on a fence rail while they admired the new hog. LeRoy noted that while he was there, "We looked a little, and we snorted a little, looked a little, and snorted a little and by ten o'clock neither of us could get back up the hill." After a pause to let this sink in, he added somewhat ruefully, " In ret-tro-spect, we should have looked more and snorted less." He didn't seem too contrite, and I suspect that he may have made more than one trip to see the boar!

A Small Garden

As LeRoy pointed out to me on one visit, nature is peculiar in its timing. "Have you ever noticed that a woman's first pregnancy can last anywhere from a few weeks to nine months, but all of the others are always nine months. Now ain't that strange?" He told me a story about two brothers who married two sisters, one couple quite a while before the second. The second brother, wanting everything to be just right before tying the knot, had built a fine cottage, a barn, and several outbuildings. He had also put in a rather small garden out back. The wedding finally took place, and it wasn't too long afterwards that the first baby arrived, considerably short of nine months. The community threw a party for the new couple and the new arrival, and LeRoy and his wife were invited. As luck would have it, LeRoy happened to overhear several of the neighborhood women discussing the affair. The first woman noted, "Now ain't this the nicest place you ever saw? Such a pretty little house, a barn and all them outbuildings. But you know, the garden's pert small, even for just two." Whereupon a second woman observed, "Well, any woman who can conjure up a full-growed baby in 6 months don't need a real big garden."

Pokey

George, LeRoy's friend down in Ceres, had become ill with pneumonia, and Leroy went down to pay him a visit. George had married a woman from southern West Virginia by the name of Pocahontas, nicknamed Pokey. LeRoy and George were sitting on the front porch when George became more short of breath and called out, "Pokey, Pokey, come here quick."

Pokey came out directly, and George told her, "Pokey, I'm in bad shape, call Doc Kegley. I can't get a long breath."

She replied "Well, George, you'll just have to take two short ones 'til he gets here."

I don't know if George managed the two short breaths for a long one until Dr. Kegley got there, but LeRoy certainly enjoyed the conversation.

A Short Horse

One spring day LeRoy told me he had planted a field of corn to feed his few head of livestock. A few months later he was in the office and mentioned that he had picked the entire field in less than a day. I told him I thought that was pretty fast even for a "small field," but flashing his wry grin he replied, "A short horse is easy curried." It has become one of my favorite expressions.

Appreciation

Bland County, Virginia was blessed with one of the most colorful physicians I have ever known. Dr. Gregory Kepler was and is a legend in this area and even had a medical facility named for him after his death. He was the epitome of the old country doctor, and many a current resident of Bland County has Dr. Kepler's name on their birth certificate. He will be remembered for his abrupt nature and his tendency to "cuss with every breath." Having developed a case of bronchitis, LeRoy happened to meet Dr. Kepler in town, and said, "Doc, I'm right sick, and I just can't get a good breath."

Dr. Kepler replied, "Why, hell, LeRoy, the problem with you is you just ain't appropriately thankful for what damned breath you can get!"

Earl

LeRoy once told me a story about Earl, a Bland County farmer whose fondness for the contents of "the mason jar" frequently got him in trouble with the legal system, as he would drive around in his old pickup truck when he had been drinking. Since he was well known to the local constabulary, and the country roads were mostly empty and slowly traveled, Earl was felt to be innocuous, and they quite frequently looked the other way. But eventually, Earl had a fender-bender that could not be overlooked, and he wound up in court on a charge of driving under the influence. The judge suspended his license for a while and told Earl that when his permit was restored, he was not to drive when he had been nipping. LeRoy said that since Earl had been driving the pickup when he had been caught, he took the judge's instructions to apply only to the truck and not to his car. Now, since the sheriff was aware of the judge's ruling and Earl's proclivities, he was on the lookout for recidivism, and one day apprehended Earl getting out of his car in front of the Western Auto store. On this occasion, the judge informed Earl that his prior decree included not only trucks, but cars and other passenger vehicles as well.

LeRoy said that things went well for a time, but one day the judge was in his chambers in the Bland County courthouse when he spied Earl weaving down the street on his old farm tractor. Enough was enough, and the judge immediately dispatched the court bailiff to haul poor Earl before him once again. This time he told Earl that the driving restriction applied to the farm tractor as well. At this point, Earl took up riding a bicycle.

LeRoy paused in his recitation and favored me with a grin. He allowed as how he felt that Earl would soon tire of the bicycle, especially not being able to ride it while inebriated, and he would most likely be caught again for some offence related to driving under the influence. Sure enough, it was not much later that I heard that a man had been arrested in Bland County for reckless endangerment of the public by riding a lawn mover down the middle of the road while under the influence of alcohol. Earl had struck again!

The Stave Barrel

Because of his chronic lung disease, I saw LeRoy frequently for bronchitis and other respiratory illnesses. On one visit he told me, "My chest feels like an old stave barrel with the all of the hoops loose." Country folks will understand this analogy, but city people may have to do some research. I had him take off his shirt, and I put my stethoscope down low on his chest, and asked him to take a deep breath. He took a shallow one and said, "Doc, I just can't get it down that far. Move 'er up a little more and I'll accommodate you."

Unique Chimes

One snowy winter day LeRoy came to the office, again for bronchitis, but he was grinning from ear to ear, and I knew he had a story to tell. Evidently a young woman he knew was living with her grandparents. She was soon to get married and had bought a new grandfather clock, which she had temporarily placed in the hallway near the bathroom. Her fiancée came to visit shortly thereafter, and she took him to see the new clock. Unfortunately, her grandfather was on the toilet and had left the bathroom door open. About the time they walked into the hall, her grandfather stood up, turned around and flushed the noisy old toilet. The girl was terribly embarrassed, but LeRoy said the boyfriend saved the day by saying, "Well, I've seen longer pendulums, and I've seen heavier weights, but the chimes are surely unique."

Still Grinning

LeRoy has since passed away, but his memory and his reputation will live on as I retell these stories to any gathering of folks who appreciate the nature of country living and the spunk of one chronically ill man who saw humor in the mundane world around him. Wherever he may be, I suspect that LeRoy's grins are still wry and his eyes are still twinkling.

Miss Viv

If LeRoy Umbarger was my favorite male humorist, Mrs. Vivian Miller was his female counterpart. Miss Viv was a widow; her husband, Colonel Miller (Colonel was his first name; he had never been in the military), had died years before I met her. She came from a large family, and as the family expanded she assumed the care of her brothers and essentially raised them into adulthood. Her maternal instincts extended to me as well, and she once told me, "I respect you as my doctor, I appreciate you as my friend, and I love you as my little boy." I did not mind the accolades at all, and the feelings, as they applied, were mutual.

Candy Bars

Miss Viv was compulsive about her medical care, and she never failed to make her appointments. She also always brought me a candy bar "to keep you sweet." On one occasion I was delayed getting into the room to see her. When I did open the door, she snapped, "Get your ass in here. I'm about to starve. I've already had to eat your candy bar." And from that day on, if I was slow getting to see her, she ate the candy bar herself, as much to admonish me for my tardiness as to satisfy her hunger!

Deafness

Miss Viv, having raised her brothers, was no stranger to bathroom humor. She once told me, "I am getting so deaf, I can't hear myself fart. If I didn't smell it, I wouldn't know I'd done it." At the same visit, she told me that her arthritis was acting up. When I asked her where she had pain, she said, "I hurt all over more than anywhere else."

Planting

As with many people in southwest Virginia, Miss Viv's father worked on the Norfolk and Western railroad and was home only on the weekends. When he left on Monday morning, he would leave a number of jobs for the children to do. One spring day, he instructed the children to plant a pumpkin seed beside each corn stalk in the rather large garden. They started out planting a seed by each corn stalk, but as they grew tired of planting the seeds, they stretched out the planting to every second plant and finally every third plant. When they got to the end of the patch they had a lot of seeds left over, and thought to conceal their duplicity by throwing the rest of the seeds in an old hollow stump. Not too long afterwards, she and the rest of the children answered their father's bellowed command to come to the garden. There they found him standing by the stump, which by now was covered with bright green leaves as the pumpkin seeds had all sprouted and were growing in great profusion from the rotten stump. They got a stern lecture about cheating and lying, but Miss Viv said they got the last laugh as the stump vines produced more and better pumpkins than any other vine in the garden.

The Scenic Route

On one occasion, Miss Viv complained of difficulty swallowing, and I referred her to Dr. Bill Deal, our general surgeon, for an EGD, a procedure to look down the esophagus with a special instrument. As she was getting prepared for the procedure, a nurse came into the room and gave her a gown telling her to take everything off, even her panties. Miss Viv, in surprise, said, "What's he planning to do, take the scenic route?" The nurse later told me that she had to leave the room before she choked on her laughter.

Getting Used to It

As Miss Viv got older she didn't keep house as well as when she was younger, and some of her friends told her the house was dirty. I thought that she might have been offended, but she told me that comments like that didn't bother her a bit. She said "You know, pretty soon I'll be covered in six feet of dirt, so I might as well get used to it now!"

I'm Not Dead Yet

One morning when I arrived in the office my nurse asked, "Did Mrs. Vivian Miller die? I heard on the radio this morning that she had." I had not heard the news, but told her that one way to find out was to call her home. I dialed her number, and after a few rings she answered the phone, and I said "Good morning, Miss Viv, this is Dr. Booker."

She said "Good morning to you too, and hell, no, I'm not dead." It seems there were two Mrs. Vivian Millers, and, even though it was the other one who had died, my Miss Viv was getting frustrated with all of the people calling to see if she was dead.

Preaching

In the early days of my private practice, I dressed very formally in coat and tie and an occasional suit. One day Miss Viv told me that I looked like a preacher. I told her my grandmother, who was a staunch Southern Baptist, always wanted me to be a preacher, but when I graduated from medical school, she accepted that I was probably saving souls in an earthly way, and that was okay for her grandson, especially as there had been seven physicians in the family background. Miss Viv asked me if I would preach at her funeral, and I jokingly said that I would. She held me to it, and when she died the family requested me to give the eulogy. In light of her personality, I told the family I was not going to engage in a dirge, and so I spent my allotted time relating the stories above. The minister in charge of the proceedings did not appreciate my remarks, apparently feeling that sort of talk was improper in "the house of the Lord" and huffed and snorted through the entire talk. Many attendees, however, commented that they had thoroughly enjoyed the anecdotes and how like Miss Viv they were. I suspect that even now Miss Viv, like Leroy, is sparking up someone's life in the hereafter.

The End

At the end of each visit to me, she would leave saying, "Just keep me going until I see you again." I did pretty well until her last visit, and then I failed her. I expect that when I see her again, she will have eaten the candy bar.

Mispronunciations
(Intentional and Otherwise)

The field of medicine, like most professions and occupations, has its own particular jargon. In fact, physicians may be the ultimate jargon-mongers. It has been estimated that the average American's useful vocabulary is about 10,000 words. In our medical training we learn over 20,000 new words, and as we become fluent in this new medical language, we toss it around with abandon, not stopping to think that our patients do not have the background to understand these words and terms. Many times this results in the words being returned to us in a much distorted form. Alzheimer's disease is one such term. Terry told me that he knew that his mother had Alzheimer's disease because she was confused all of the time. He reckoned he had "halfheimer's disease" because he was confused only half the time. He said he bought some ginkgo biloba to help his memory, but he forgot to take it half the time. Kenny told me he had "sometimer's disease;" sometimes he could remember and sometimes he couldn't. Henry felt that he had "parttimer's disease;" part of the time he could remember and part of the time he couldn't. Mrs. Davidson, who was 88 years old, was serious when she said her sister was having trouble with her memory and thought she had "oldtimer's disease."

There are many other distortions that I have collected over the years, most from my own experience, but a number have come from other sources. Dr. Stone said that Nettie told him that her husband, Earley, was on the "perspirator" (ventilator) in the "expensive care unit," and she did not expect him to live. She said that if he died she wanted to "cremolate" (cremate) him.

My son, Jake, who is a gynecologist, had a patient who had undergone a "culinary by-pass" (coronary by-pass).

Bobby was riding his bicycle when he developed diverticulitis and was hospitalized. Later when I saw him in the office he described in great detail his ordeal with "bicyclulitis."

Sodium and potassium are called electrolytes, and occasionally they become imbalanced, which can cause the onset of atrial fibrillation (a heart-rhythm disturbance). One of my patients told me he had developed "electric light imbalance and new onsite April affiliation."

Another patient who had been seen in the emergency room with a fractured kneecap (patella) later told me she had suffered "a broken propeller."

In talking with a family member about a patient who was very sick, I mentioned that he was "in extremis" (very seriously ill), whereupon the person huffily replied that the patient was most certainly "not an extremist," he was just real sick.

One of Dr. Stone's patients told him that her brother had just suffered a "master" stroke (massive stroke) and was in the hospital on an "aspirator" (ventilator) and another said her son had "strack throak" (strep throat).

Here are a number of variations on "hiatal hernia":

High layer hernia
High hernia
High enial hernia

And for "inguinal hernia":

In queenal hernia
Enial herndon
Congenial hernia
Ingenial hernia
Ingenital hernia

A patient with varicose veins had a bad case of "very close veins" and another had "vertical veins."

Mrs. Kittle's daughter had "anal fishes" (anal fissure) and Katherine didn't take her temperature because she had lost her "mometer" (thermometer).

One of Dr. Stone's patients wanted some "suppucatories" (suppositories) for her "hemagroids" (hemorrhoids).

A patient whose daughter had schizophrenia and frequent mood swings had "skip-a-phrenia" and Mrs. Clark's mother had trouble breathing because of "asmie." (asthma)

Mr. Henry was treated for bronchitis. On a return visit some months later he told me he had that "chitis" again. When I asked what he meant, he said, "You know, that brown chitis." Another chronic lung disease patient told me he had "badchitis."

A patient with fibrocystic disease of the breast told me she had "fibrobreastic cysts," (fibrocystic disease) and John complained of frequent "sinu-nitis" (sinusitis).

Mrs. Sage told Dr. Stone that she had the "copper-handle syndrome " (carpal tunnel syndrome) in her wrists.

When I asked Mr. George about his family history, he told me his father had died with "dramatic fever" (rheumatic fever) and Marsha told me that she had been diagnosed with early "masculine degeneration" (macular degeneration) in her right eye.

Mr. Cullop told me his heart was racing and that he needed a "KGB" (EKG), and Mrs. Sharitz said she needed a "heartogram" (cardiogram).

Mrs. Neel told me her sister was in the hospital with "hypercation" (dehydration) and was getting "blucose" (glucose) in the vein.

Mr. Pattison had been to the ophthalmologist to have his "cadillacs" (cataracts) removed, and Mrs. Compton complained of "brutalitis" (bursitis) in her right shoulder. (I suspect that anyone who has had acute bursitis of the shoulder would agree with her pronunciation!)

Mrs. Rorrer said that her hip had been hurting and wondered if "hip-nosis" would work. And "monster-itis" masqueraded as mastoiditis, which is an infection in the mastoid bone behind the ear.

Charlie told me that his mother had died of "monia," but he did not know whether it was old or new (pneumonia).

Mr. Tate came to see me because of "electron bursitis" (olecranon bursitis) in the right elbow, and Mr. Samuel had worsening "conversation" (congestion) in his chest.

Mr. Akers told me his brother had been diagnosed with "reptile malfunction" (erectile dysfunction) and was taking "niagra" (Viagra), which made him urinate a lot.

At age 96, Mr. Aker told me he had been faithfully using his "peter meter" and that he was really proud of his readings. When I asked him how it read, he said "In miles, of course." (pedometer)

Victor, an old cattle farmer, told me how his bull, in chasing a cow, had jumped a fence, but not quite cleared it and had broken his "pendulum." (penis)

Mrs. Huddle had the typical fall seasonal allergy and told me she had a "sneezonal allergy," whereas George told me he had such pain in his knees that he thought he had "kneesles."

Mrs. Jones had to be operated on for "adhesures" (adhesions), Mrs. Vaught had been given "transilizers" (tranquilizers) for her nerves, and Mrs. Manley had a bad case of "shangles" (shingles).

Della told me that she had developed an infection in her "belly eye." Being unaware of, but two eyes, both in the head, I asked her to show me. She forthwith pulled up her blouse and showed me the redness and drainage from her navel.

And lastly, Mrs. Hancock, whose family helped run a local dairy farm, told me she had too much "ensilage," Wondering why too much silage would be a problem on a dairy farm, I asked her how that affected her and she said, "Why, honey, it drops my sugar too low!" (insulin)

Quips and Quotes

Some of my greatest chuckles have come on the heels of greeting a patient as I walk into the examining room and getting a one liner in return. One of my favorites came from Harry, a mortician, who, when I asked, "Hi, Harry, how's business?" replied, "Dead!"

When I greeted Mrs. Rose, who was ninety-five years old, she told me, "I'm not sick; I'm old. Can you do anything about old?"

Mrs. Burchett said, "I'm old and gray and just in the way."

Mrs. Patrick said, "If I was fine, I wouldn't be here!"

Henry said, "I must be doing okay; my grave is still empty."

And several patients bested the old saw, "I'm as fine as frog hair" with "I'm as fine as frog hair split four ways."

It amuses me when a patient replies affirmatively, by asking another question. One example is Paul. When I asked if he were still taking his blood-pressure medicine he borrowed a medical term and replied, "Do bears defecate in the woods?"

One of the best came when I asked a patient if he would like samples of his medication. He said "Would a cow lick Lot's wife?"

Many one liners come when patients tell me how busy they are. Most of us have heard the expression, "I'm as busy as a one-armed paper hanger," the humor coming from the mental image generated by that situation. Here are a few choice endings I've heard for "I'm as busy as…":

"a dung beetle in a cattle barn."

"bullets in a war zone."

"a maggot in a meat house."

"a blade of grass in a hurricane."
"a belly over a jackhammer."

Perseverance has been the subject of a few zingers, usually phrased with an addendum to "I'm hanging in there, like…":

"a fly on a biscuit."
"white on snow."
"stink on a skunk."
"black on tarpaper."
"stripes on a tiger."
"fuzzy on an ape."
"a mite on a woodpecker's head."

Most of the best quips occur in individual settings, but some deal with the same subject. Bowlegs have resulted in two replies, the first coming from Fred Smith, a little short fellow, who told me that if he wasn't "so bowlegged he would be six feet tall." Mrs. Patrick told me about a lady she knew who was so bowlegged "she couldn't hem a hog in a ditch."

And this one also about Mrs. Patrick, who was cancerophobic, came from her granddaughter, who told her, "Grandma, if you don't die of cancer, you'll die of disappointment!"

Most of the one-liners I have collected came at odd times in taking a medical history or just talking to patients in general. They occurred in no particular context and just came out of the blue. I have chosen the best of the best in the following pages. I trust that the reader will appreciate them as much as I have enjoyed collecting and retelling them.

Mr. Gordon, who had Alzheimer's disease, told me, "I still do everything that I used to do; I just don't know why I do it." He also said, "If you tell me what I was supposed to do, I'll tell you whether or not I'm doing it."

Mary Ella said, *In Memoriam,* a radio daily obituary, was her favorite program. "I'm always glad when I don't hear my name."

Tony said that he had been told he had suffered a heart attack, but he said, "Doc, I've got a good heart; it wouldn't attack me."

Tom told me that his wife had "combined systems disease, PMS and ESP; she's grouchy as hell and knows everything."

Harry told me that the only thing golden about his golden years was his urine.

Sandy said that she had started dieting and walking because she needed to get a "tiny hiney."

Mrs. Rhudy couldn't believe the cost of her urinalysis. "Why, I just brought in a tiny little bit!"

A Baptist minister who was a patient on the medical floor asked his nurse, Larry, if he was saved. Larry replied, "Why, hell yes, Reverend, I ain't taking no damned chances."

Charlie said he was so old he remembered "when the Dead Sea got sick."

Mr. Houseman asked me one day, "Have you ever noticed how people try to get well before they go to a doctor so he won't find anything wrong?"

Mr. Rash observed, "The last good night's sleep a man has is the night before his first child is born."

Gladys told me she had found the secret to everlasting life. "I'll never die; I'm too fat to get through the pearly gates."

When I asked Fred if he drank alcohol he replied, "Once in the morning and a little while in the afternoon."

The landlord had raised Mrs. Morrow's rent, and she told me, "I would move out of this town if it weren't for my doctor and my beautician."

I was frustrated with Charlie's continued smoking, and I asked him, "Charlie, whenever are you going quit smoking?"

Without hesitation, he replied, "In two years next month."

When I asked him how he could be so specific, he said, "That's when my boss is retiring!"

Mr. Bowers, a two-pack-per-day smoker who had coronary artery disease and chronic lung disease and had suffered two strokes, said, "But the smoking don't bother me!"

In a similar vein, Mr. Spence had smoked since age eight and suffered from heart disease, arterial disease, venous disease, stasis leg ulcers, and stomach ulcers, but stated that smoking didn't bother him because, "I don't have any trouble breathing!"

A deer smashed right into the front of Roger's new SUV. His wife, Audrey, didn't help matters when she told him, "At least you won't go hungry with all of that grilled venison!"

Mrs. Bralley told me, "When I try to quit smoking, I get so nervous, my hands get in my way."

Al told me that he wanted to be buried at Wal Mart, "so my wife will visit me every day."

Mrs. Metz, at age ninety-one, was being examined for rectal bleeding. My nurse, Polly, said, "Slide your tail down the table."

Mrs. Metz said, "Shall I wag it, too?"

Mr. Akers was chronically ill and told me he realized he was living on borrowed time. On one visit he said, "I just came in today to borrow a little more time."

Miss Vergie, a homebody, was going to visit her daughter in New Jersey. She said, "Now doctor, you know, I ain't gonna see any doctors up there, so you call me every day and tell me how I'm feeling."

"How are you feeling, Mrs. Stroud?" I asked.

"Well, I thought I was feeling good, but the nurse told me I wasn't."

Mrs. Jones told me she had undergone a cholecystectomy, appendectomy, tonsillectomy and adenoidectomy, and a hysterectomy. She said, "I've had so much taken out, I'm all heart."

When I asked Mrs. McQueen if she was still smoking, she quipped, "Not when I'm asleep." It reminded me of Mark Twain who said that he smoked only once a day...all day long!

Ray said he had been exercising a lot. When I asked him what he did, he said "I run around in circles and jump to conclusions."

Life seemed to be going by awfully fast for Bucky, who said that life is like a roll of toilet paper: "The closer you get to the end, the faster it goes."

One of Mr. Cassel's neighbors was tri-lingual, "English, profanity and vulgarity."

Mrs. Neese said her sister was a hypochondriac, and "If she doesn't have any problems today, she'll tell you what hurt yesterday."

Dr. Stone told Stephanie that if she didn't have anything to worry about, she would worry about not having anything to worry about.

Our lab and x-ray tech, Debbie, took a trip from the mountains of southwest Virginia to the Midwest, where the prairie made a big impression on her. She told me, "It's so flat out there you can see a dog running away for three miles."

When she stumbled over a stool, Dr. Stone's nurse, Debbie, exclaimed, "I'm as clumsy as an anvil out of water."

When I asked Mrs. Mustard if she had a bad taste in her mouth, she said, "Now where else would I have a bad taste?"

Mr. Webb told Dr. Stone that he didn't mind getting old. "I just don't want to get ugly."

Janet told me, "Most people eat to live; I live to eat."

Dr. Stone's patient, Mrs. Webb, said, "I'm getting so frail and thin, I have to drink muddy water just to cast a shadow."

Dr. Stone asked one of his elderly women who had been ill if her stamina was coming back. She replied, "No, but my niece is coming tomorrow."

Mrs. Neel had advanced arthritis, especially in her hands. She told me her hands looked so bad, "I told Bill Grubb [the undertaker] to bury me with my hands behind me."

When Dr. Stone asked a teenager, "What are you up to these days?" he replied, "About 5' 6"."

Carson came to see me about chest pain, which he did not feel was anything of concern, but he came anyway because he had gotten tired of listening to his wife's "chin music."

Mrs. James told me that the best thing about menopause was that "You don't have to take any crap off anybody."

When I mentioned to Don that he was really overweight he told me that he had been poisoned. "Poisoned?" I asked.

"Yep, biscuit poisoning."

A favorite expression in our part of the country for having to do a job over, "I'll just have to lick the calf again."

When I asked Bill what he did for a living, he said he owned a septic-tank pumping service, and added, "It's a crappy way to make a living!"

My nurse, Robin, told me about a patient who had "summer teeth...some were in and some weren't."

When I suggested female hormone therapy to an elderly woman, she said, "My god, Doctor, they'll have to bury me with a Kotex on."

Tammy told me she had the Sealy Syndrome. "I can't get out of bed in the morning."

While I was doing a genital exam on Don, he told me he had a "frilly dilly" because he had been circumcised with pinking shears.

Mrs. Lootens had lost one of her hearing aids and could "only hear half" of what I said.

Mary Ella's niece said that she had been raped, but Mary Ella said it was a lie because, "Any fool knows a girl can run faster with her dress up than a man can with his pants down."

Both Bob and Cecile told me that "What doesn't hurt, doesn't work."

Mark told me that what hair wasn't "turning grey was turning loose."

Diane said she had a breakfast body: "My buns are like pancakes, my breasts are like fried eggs, and my belly is like a ham."

Reggie felt so bad it was like he had been "trampled by a slow-moving herd of turtles."

Mr. Eversole was ninety-two years old when he told me he needed to take care of himself so he could "live to be an old man."

When Brenda told her husband, Bo, that she had gotten him a pair of Clark's shoes, he asked, "Well, what's he wearing?"

Dale had her husband on a low-fat diet. She had fed him so much chicken that when it got dark he started "looking for a roost."

Sue had urinary incontinence and called to make an appointment with the urologist. The receptionist, apparently busy, answered, "Urology Associates. Can you hold a moment?"

Sue replied, "If I could hold it, I wouldn't be calling you."

When I asked James how old he was he said, "As old as my tongue and a little older than my teeth."

Old Mr. Eversole had been a well driller all his life. As he got older, he didn't sleep well and dreamed a lot. One day when I asked him if he had drilled any wells lately he said, "Doc, I've drilled a well every night for the last year."

Dr. Stone asked a patient how she felt. She replied, "I feel fine. Any day above dirt is a good day."

I congratulated Reed on turning seventy. He said, "Doc, you've heard the old saying 'the older the bull, the harder the horn?' Well, it ain't true!"

When Mr. Chandler came to the office for a truck-driver physical exam, I asked him his full name. He said "Carrington Lloyd Chandler. With a name like that I should have been a damned lawyer instead of a concrete-truck driver!"

Katlyn had such a bad case of diarrhea that her mother said the commode turned "fluorescent green and glowed in the dark."

Randolph called his diabetic orthopedic shoes "sugar shoes."

Ron described his erectile dysfunction as "it's not as long or as strong as it ought to be."

Danny, who had urinary frequency, said that he had "short kidneys."

John told me of a woman he worked with who went to have a mammogram. She told the technician that she did not have much to work with and wanted a fifty-percent discount on the bill.

Another patient who had undergone a left mastectomy, went to have a mammogram on the right breast. She asked the technician if she would get "half off." She was assured that it was, indeed, "half off," and no pun was intended!

This story came to me third hand from my patient, Linda, who told me about a woman who, when asked if she was incontinent, replied, "Why, yes. I live right here in town."

Bud came in for his annual physical, and as I was reviewing his history, I asked him about his bowel movements. He said he was as regular as clockwork, every morning at 7:00, but he added, "Problem is, I don't get up until 8:30!"

Deanna complained that she had "taken a cold." She said, "You know, growing up poor, I'll take whatever anybody will give me."

Viagra gets a lot of attention by my patients. Johnny told me that he got a Viagra pill stuck in his throat and had a stiff neck for a week. Old Carlton said he took a half pill of Viagra each morning just so he wouldn't pee on his shoes. Gary said he soaked earthworms in Viagra and used them for nails. The problem was when the effect wore off the building fell down.

And finally, I asked Trish what she did for a living. She replied, "I piss people off. I'm a claims adjuster, and I read them the fine print!"

Come Again?

As patients try to answer our questions, they sometimes take a very circuitous route to get to what they want to say. Age, medicines, acute illness, difficulty hearing, and occasionally alcohol, etc. all have a bearing on these conversations. Sometimes it is difficult to ascertain exactly what the patient means and sometimes it is very clear, but expressed in a humorous way. Like the day when I asked Dan how he was feeling. He replied, "I'm doing better now than I was before I got worse." I still haven't figured that one out. The following stories are straight from patient encounters, either my own or told to me by other health-care workers. I trust that you will enjoy them as much as I did initially and as much as I do now in retelling them

Nothing on TV

I was working in the emergency room one night when an elderly man was brought in with shortness of breath and slightly inebriated. The conversation went like this:

"What brings you to the emergency room this evening?"
"The ambulance."
"Okay. What seems to be the problem?"
"I'se sick."
"What's the matter?"
"That's what I came to find out."
"Well, can you tell me how you feel?"
"Bad."
"Can you tell me what's wrong?"

"That's what you're supposed to find out."

"Well, you have to give me something to go on."

"I'se drunk as a skunk, I can't breathe, my back hurts, I can't pee, I'm dizzy and there ain't nothing on TV."

With that, I just gave up and started doing a physical exam.

The Fall

My nurse, Robin Dalton, brought Mrs. Morris back to the exam room, and while taking her vital signs asked, "Mrs. Morris, how did you fall?"

She huffily replied, "That woman at the front desk asked me the same thing. Why are you all asking me about falling?"

Robin said, "Well, that's what's written on your chart. But it really doesn't matter what you are here for; I just need to let the doctor know why you are here. What should I tell him?"

She said, "That I fell!"

Right Now

Mrs. Richardson phoned in to the office and was talking to nurse, Robin. "Robin, I've got to see Dr. Booker right now. I've got chest pain and shortness of breath. I'm dizzy as a coot, and my legs are swollen something terrible. My blood pressure is eighty over forty, and I can't walk a step."

This sounded pretty bad, so Robin told her to come right on in, and we would see her as soon as she got there.

Mrs. Richardson replied, "Lord, honey, I can't come now, I've got errands to run."

In a similar vein, Katherine called and left a message on Robin's voice mail that she was so weak and sick, she couldn't even get out of her chair. She asked Robin to call her back "real quick," because she was leaving for Bible School.

Which One?

At one time in Wytheville, Virginia, there were two shopping centers at opposite ends of town, both with Super-X pharmacies beside Food Lion grocery stores. This led to some confusion at times, but none as acute as when Debra Jean called wanting a prescription called in for her. "Robin, I need some cough medicine called to the drug store."

"I think Dr. Booker will do that for you, which drug store do you use?"

"The Super-X."

"Which one?'

"The one by Food Lion."

"Which Food Lion?"

"The one on the end of town."

"Which end of town?"

"The one where the shopping center is."

"Which shopping center?"

"The one with the Super-X in it."

Next Week

I had just gotten back from vacation when Mrs. Corvin called Robin and said that she needed to see me "next week." Robin checked the schedule and told her to come in Tuesday of next week. From there the conversation went:

"Next week? Honey, I need to see him today."

"But you said you wanted to see him next week."

"I know, but I think I need to see him today."

"Well, okay. Come on in now, and we will work you in."

"Now, honey? Lord, I can't get there now."

"Well, you said you need to be seen today."

"Oh, well, okay. I'll find somebody to bring me in today, but what am I going to do about next week?"

A Rack

Miss Vergie was an interesting little woman whom I took care of for years. She was not well versed in current events, and as she got older, her hearing became progressively worse. In August of 1990 during the Iraq war she came to the office where I engaged her in conversation thusly:

"Miss Vergie, what do you think of that business in Iraq?"
"Why, I didn't put nothing on a rack."
"No, No. Iraq."
"I don't even have a rack."
Robin said, "Miss Vergie, he's talking about the Persian Gulf."
"Why, yes, honey, I praise God all the time."
We ended the conversation there without ever learning if Miss Vergie knew about Iraq or not.

Wandaisms

Wanda was schizophrenic and sometimes had trouble with the obvious, as illustrated by the following two observations:

"I can't see in the dark unless there's a light on."
"I don't know why I'm sick. I always stay at home unless I'm somewhere else."

Huh?

I admitted Mrs. Stroud with chest pain that turned out to be a heart attack. When I asked her what the pain felt like, she replied, "Like my other six heart attacks."
I asked, "Can you describe what the pain feels like?"
She said, "Like the last three, but not like the first one and certainly not like the second one."
I asked, "What did the last three feel like?"

She said, "Just like this one."
I never did learn the particular characteristics of any of them.

Take Two

My partner, Dr. Wayne Horney, told me of one of his patients who had gone to the GNC store to get some Vitamin B-12, but the store had sold out of all the B-12 products. The saleslady, trying to be helpful suggested, "Why don't you buy a bottle of the B-6 capsules and just take two of those!"

Now That's a Trick

Mrs. Davidson came to see me because of discomfort in the right leg. She was having difficulty describing the pain, but finally decided that "the inside of my leg is longer than the outside."

I'll Try to Be There

Mr. Houseman worked at the Southwestern State mental hospital in Marion, Virginia, and told me this tale of an inmate who had "bad anemia." He told Mr. Houseman that he was "going to die tomorrow" and that the funeral would be three days later. He asked if Mr. Houseman would be there, and Mr. Houseman assured him that if he did die, he would certainly be at the funeral. He then asked the man if he, too, planned to be there. The man replied in all seriousness, "Well, I don't know yet, I've got some other plans, but I'm going to try to make it."

Going to Die

Sometimes even the most distressing situations hold elements of humor, especially if the outcome is favorable, as it was in this story.

In our hospital, any person who attempts suicide or makes a suicide gesture is admitted to the intensive care unit and watched carefully and attentively until the crisis is resolved. One evening, I was called by the emergency-room physician for a woman who had gotten into a spat with her boyfriend, and who had taken an overdose of sleeping pills. I asked him to admit her to the intensive care unit and to implement suicide precautions. When I arrived a little later, the crisis had passed, since the boyfriend had come in, and they had mended their feud. As I was finishing up my work, the nurse came in to tell me that during her initial evaluation, she had asked the patient why she had taken the overdose. The woman had replied, "My boyfriend left me. Life's not worth living anymore. I want to die."

As tactfully as possible, the nurse asked, "If you wanted to die from the overdose, why did you come to the emergency room instead of staying home?"

The woman said, "Well, my chest started hurting, and I thought I was going to die!"

Retribution

I was not in the office on Thursday, which was the day Glenna came to the office and had to wait 3 ½ hours to be worked in to see one of my partners. That night her daughter called me, most irate, and demanded to know why her mother had to wait so long to see a physician. I explained to her that I had not been in the office and did not know the reason for the delay. She again demanded an explanation, and I once again told her that I was not there and could not tell her. The longer we talked, the more frustrated she became and finally said, "You have the most terrible office I've ever seen! It would serve your right if my mother gets pneumonia and dies!" And with that she hung up! I am sure she did not mean what came out, and that is the reason this anecdote is included in the section of "Come again?"

A Strange Insomnia

Mildred called me during office hours to tell me that her husband had a terrible toothache, and she had not slept for two nights. Since it was her husband with the toothache, I asked her why she could not sleep. She said that since her husband would not allow her to sleep in the bed, she had to sit in a chair and could not go to sleep. I then asked her why her husband would not allow her in the bed, and she reckoned that it must have made his toothache worse. I then asked how he slept if she was not in the bed with him and she replied, "Oh, he sleeps just fine if I'm not there. Do you think that's unusual or strange?"

Well, I certainly did think it was strange, but to avoid further lines of inquiry during my busy day, I told her that toothaches were the bailiwick of the dentists and to call theirs forthwith. I did suggest that she stick to the toothache and leave out the insomnia part.

Miss Alma

Miss Alma was ninety-nine years old when she told me, "I've lived three lives already. I remember the first two better than the third, and I am looking forward to the fourth more than any of the others."

And with that, I will end this section of anecdotes.

Mrs. Fussbudget

Mrs. Fussbudget was the most aggravating, irritating, and frustrating patient I have ever met. She was obese and slovenly. Her personal hygiene left something to be desired, and her piercing, screeching, nasally drawl would irritate even the most tolerant of physicians. She had an uncanny ability to irritate even before one got to know her and to irritate even more when one did get to know her. She took no responsibility for her own health care and criticized and reviled anyone who recommended any changes in her habits that would result in better health. She whined and complained that no one listened to her, but when anyone did attempt to minister to her, she complained that they insulted her or, in some other way offended her. Her longsuffering husband, rest his soul, was apparently able to overcome her persona, but not the dementia to which he eventually succumbed. His last years were spent enduring the acid tongue of his wife, who reviled him at every turn and even wondered aloud why "he couldn't just go on and die and get it over with."

Thankfully, I was not her primary provider, happily leaving that odious task to one of my partners, who tolerated her with a heaven-inspired patience. I did, however, have to see her occasionally when her physician was absent. Once, in trying to deal with her morbid obesity, I suggested that reducing her food portions might be helpful. She thereupon informed me that her condition was "genetic" and that there was nothing she or anyone else could do to change that unfortunate combination of chromosomal particles.

Assuming my role as health educator, I tried to explain the relationship between caloric intake and energy expenditure, but she said, "I told you, this is genetic, and besides, I do watch everything I eat."

In frustration, I acknowledged that I was sure she did, indeed, watch everything she ate, from her plate right into her mouth. Needless to say, the office visit went downhill from there, and she left no better educated and considerably more acerbic. Later, after she had seen my partner in follow-up, he told me that I had thoroughly insulted her and that she refused to ever see me again. After a thoughtful pause he added, "You did that on purpose, didn't you?"

Not too long afterward, she developed, not unexpectedly, a heart problem and was referred to our local cardiologist. After a few visits, he, not unexpectedly, attempted to return her to our care, using multiple untenable medical machinations to accomplish this even to the point of sending us a consultation form noting that "Mrs. Fussbudget requests the honor of your presence at a private candlelight dinner in her hospital room!" Not to be outdone, I spent an enjoyable two hours paraphrasing a basic American document declaring our independence and freedom from tyranny, stated thusly:

A Declaration of Medical Independence

When in the Course of medical events, it becomes necessary for Physicians to dissolve the doctor-patient bonds which have connected them with one another, and to assume among the powers of the earth, the separate and equal station to which the Laws of Nature and of Nature's God entitle them, a decent respect to the opinions of other Physicians requires that they should declare the causes which impel them to the separation.

We hold these truths to be self-evident that some patients will drive a Physician to distraction, that they are endowed by their Creator with certain unalienable Rights, that among them are whining, complaining, and the pursuit of hypochondria.

That whenever these patient Rights become burdensome to the Physicians, it is the right of those Physicians to alter or abolish the union and to institute new doctor-patient relationships on such principles as to them shall seem most likely to effect their Safety, Happiness, and Peace of Mind. Prudence, indeed, will dictate that those bonds long established should not be changed for light and transient causes; and accordingly, all experience has shewn, that Physicians are more disposed to suffer, while such patients are sufferable, than to right themselves by abolishing the bonds to which they are accustomed. But when a long train of abuses, whinings, complainings, endless questions, and refusal to accept reality, pursuing invariable the same Object of avoiding personal responsibility, it is the Physicians' right, it is their duty, to throw off such attachments, and to provide new Guards for their future sanity.

Such has been the patience of these Physicians and such is now the necessity which constrains them to alter their former doctor-patient relationship. The history of the present patient is a history of repeated injuries and usurpations, all having in direct object the establishment of an absolute Tyranny over these Physicians.

Be it now known to all men, that the Physicians will henceforth seek to foster new doctor-patient relationships for said patient, preferably with specialists whose tolerability of such behavior hath been shewn to be superior in all respects to that of mere Physicians to families and whose capabilities for endless procedures, both invasive and non-invasive, provide for sufficient remuneration to such specialists as to make them more tolerant of the foibles and demands of said patients.

Mrs. Fussbudget defied nature and lived to a ripe old age, bedeviling all of her physicians right up to the end.

I Kid You Not

Some exchanges with patients are so strange they almost defy belief, but the very fact that they are so unusual provides some degree of authentification. I kid you not; these stories are true to the best of my ability to get them down on paper as soon as possible.

You'se Not Frank!

I had not been in Wytheville very long and was on call one night when the phone awoke me from a sound sleep. I usually answer such a call with, "This is Dr. Booker," but this night I just said, "Hello."

An obviously inebriated female voice shouted, "What you doin' over there, you black son of a bitch?"

Still gathering my wits, I said, "Huh?"

The voice said, "Don't you jive me, you black turkey!"

By now I realized that this was not only a wrong number, but a great opportunity, and I said, "What you talking about?"

She said, "Don't F— with me; I knows you's over dere with Catherine!"

I said, "How'd you find out I'se over here?"

She said, "I done had you followed, and I knows yo' game, you cheating bastard!"

I replied, "Listen, honey babe, you is still my number-one squeeze."

At that, there was a pause, and she said, "Hey, you ain't Frank."

I said, "No, I'se Howard."

The next sound I heard was "click." As I hung up the phone, my wife said, "What on earth was that all about?" I said, "You wouldn't believe me if I told you." To this day, I have no idea who the caller was or who Frank was, but I bet from then on, she was more careful about identifying who answered the phone!

The Bone

Charlie was not the brightest guy around, but usually he was pretty straight forward, so he really caught me off-guard one day when I went in the room with him. I wrote down this encounter as soon as I left the room so that I wouldn't forget the sequence. Here it is in its entirety:

"Where'd that bone come from, Doc?"
"What bone is that, Charlie?'
"The one I passed out of my rear end."
"You passed a bone out of your rear end?"
"Yep."
"How big was it?"
"'Bout this big" holding up two fingers, two inches apart.
"Where is it now?
"I burned it."
"You burned it?"
"Yep."
"Why'd you do that?"
"It's bad luck to pass a bone."
"It's bad luck to pass a bone?"
"Yep."
"Why's it bad luck to pass a bone, Charlie?"
"I don't know, but that's what all the old witchy women say."
"Well, if you passed a bone, it had to come from something you ate."
"The hell, you say! It must of come from that damned chicken I eat over to Tazewell on Sunday."

The conversation ended there, with Charlie hopefully learning a little about the origin of bones in the GI tract, and I certainly learning a little about the superstitions of the folks in the mountains of southwest Virginia.

I Could've Bled to Death

A serious subject by most standards, suicide can become a humorous topic in certain circumstances. Such was the case with Ryan and his multiple contacts with medical personnel over his "suicidal gestures." Suicidal gestures are a mechanism employed by people desiring attention but not knowing how to get it. They will do something that sounds and looks suicidal, but on closer medical inspection could not possibly have resulted in death. The gesture does bring multiple people running, and the patient is the center of attention, if only for a short period of time. Ryan was an atypical suicidal gesturer in that he would call the hospital or the rescue squad before such an attempt and, in time, help would arrive before he had "taken action." On one such occasion, he called the rescue squad, told them he was in the post office and was going to cut his wrists. Being aware of Ryan's prior behavior, the rescue squad was in no hurry to get there, and upon arrival, Ryan, unharmed as usual, was standing in the entrance waiting for them to get there. As they walked in he said, "Where have you guys been? I could've bled to death by now!"

Red Icing on the Cake

Miss Thelma was very much involved in the family restaurant business. Her specialty was making the desserts, especially the really fancy, decorated cakes. She came to see me one day because of spontaneous and unpredictable nosebleeds. They were getting to be a problem because, as she said, "When I'm decorating the cakes, I can't tell the blood from the red icing!" Then she grinned!

It Was the Medicine

It is illegal in Virginia to hunt from a state road, and Woody had been apprehended by a game warden for shooting a deer from the road. He came to the office requesting a note from me stating that his medicine had made him do it! I told him that there were a lot of side effects from his medicine, but that was not one of them.

Too Tired to Think—One

Every physician who has spent any time in the profession can tell stories about long hours and fatigue that render one goofy in the extreme. My cousin, Dr. Motley Booker, was an old-time country physician in the Northern Neck of Virginia. He initially installed the phone next to his bed, but because late night phone calls frequently caught him so tired that he could not remember the gist of the call, he relocated the phone out in the hall. He thought that if he had to get out of bed and walk out into the hall, he would be more likely to remember the call. This worked well until one night when he had been out all night and had gotten home about 4:30 A.M. He had just gone to sleep when the phone rang. He dragged himself out of bed, walked out into the hall and answered the phone. His wife related the rest of the story. "Hello. Dr. Booker?"

"No, I'm sorry; he hasn't gotten back yet." And he hung up the phone and went back to bed!

Too Tired to Think—Two

As noted before, Dr. Jim Stone and I started medical school together in June of 1963, and except for our brief sojourns in the military, he in the Army and I in the Air Force, we have been together ever since. Our experiences together run deep, and I have related a lot of humorous material he has given to me. This is one of the best "Jim stories." It is on him and was told to me by a nurse in the intensive-care unit. It was early one Monday morning, and Jim had been on call all weekend. He apparently had just gotten to sleep when Patsy Muncy had to notify him that his patient had just died. She related the conversation thusly:

"Hello."

"Dr. Stone, this is Patsy in the ICU. Mrs. Jones just expired."

"Well, go out to the barn and cut the lights on."

"Dr. Stone! Listen to me! Mrs. Jones just died."

Long sleepy pause. "Well, I guess we don't need to cut the lights on, then."

I Can't See

Mikey, a Baptist minister, was bald, vain, and toupeed. I doubt that even his wife ever saw him without his hairpiece. One evening he developed ureteral colic from a kidney stone and required hospitalization. His pain was severe and required large doses of morphine for comfort. On rounds the next morning I found that he had passed the stone during the night, but the residual effects of his last morphine dose had sedated him into a deep sleep. In his tossing and turning, the toupee had slipped around until the ear notch was down over his nose and the sides were draped over his eyes. I gently shook him awake, and as he came out of his stupor he exclaimed in fright, "Oh, Lord, help me! I can't see! I've gone blind!"

It was the first case and easiest case of blindness that I ever treated.

Where's the Train?

As Bill got older his memory got worse, and in a benign attempt to keep in touch with him and give him a way to get help if needed, his family decided to get him a cell phone. They insisted that he carry the phone at all times when he was out of the house. His grandson programmed the new phone and made sure that Bill understood the quick-dial features to call home or to the rescue squad if his wife did not answer. The first day he had the phone he went off to the post office, and while he was gone his wife, Betty, decided to see if the phone was working. She dialed the number and it rang and rang, but Bill did not answer. She hung up and tried several more times in succession, before giving up and deciding that he must have cut it off. When Bill got home, she asked, "Why'd you cut the phone off?"

He said, "I didn't cut the phone off; it's still on, see?"

And he showed her that it was indeed on. They then concluded that the phone must not be working properly, so Betty once again dialed the number. Instantly, the phone rang with the train whistle the grandson had programmed for the ring tone. Bill looked at the phone in amazement and said, "Well, I'll be damned; I looked out of every window in the post office for that train!"

It's a Man Thing

I was on call one night, and the emergency room referred a Mr. Fred Johnson to me for a "water problem." Apparently, he had undergone some type of prostate procedure by his urologist. The conversation went like this:

"What's the problem, Mr. Johnson?"

"It's my water."

"What's the matter with your water?"

"Well, I don't know. That's why I called you."

"How's it bothering you?"

"It's that man thing."

"Well, why did you call me?"

"I just came back from having that thing operated on."

"What thing?"

"That man thing, you know, that prostrate thing, where you can't pee."

"Oh, okay. What did they do?"

"I don't know…they just operated on it."

"Did they tell you anything about it at all?"

"Nope. I guess they did whatever you do to them things."

"Well, there are a number of things they do, and I need to know more about what they did so I can help you."

"I can't help you there. Dr. Griffin just told me I needed to be fixed and he did it, but ever since they took that thing out, my water's not been right."

"What thing did they take out?"

"That long tube thing."

"You mean the catheter?"

"I guess that's what you call it. It's long and brown and goes in a bag."

"So what happened after they took it out?"

"I can't drink water."

"You can't drink water?"

"Well, I can drink it, but iffen I do, it don't stop inside."

"What do you mean, it doesn't stop inside?"

"Why, son, it runs right through my pipes."

"You mean you can't control your bladder?"

"Well, if you mean I'm peeing all the time, I guess that's right."

"I see. When did they take the catheter out?"

"Well, it weren't there when I got home, so I guess they took it out before I left."

"When did you leave?"

"This afternoon."

"Well, if they just took it out today, you may have some leaking for a while."

"This ain't leaking, son, this is pouring! What I want to know is, will it get better?"

"Yes, sir, it usually gets better with time."

"How much time?"

"I can't say for sure. Maybe a day or two."

"Son, I can't wait too long; this house ain't but so big, but I got the doors open!"

"I understand. Did Dr. Griffin give you any medicine to take?"

"I'm taking that there Max Flow they give me before they operated on me."

"You mean, Flomax?"

"Oh, yes sir, that's it. Hey, ain't that the stuff that makes you go?"

"Yes, that is one of the medicines we use for that."

"So iffen I quit taking that, I'll get better?"

"I would think that would certainly help."

"Is there anything that I can do right now?"

"No, sir, not right now, but it should get better pretty soon."

"Oh, well, that's good. You know, there is something I can do to keep from wetting the bed until then."

"What's that?

"Sleep on the floor."

I never found out who this gentleman was. He did not know who had referred him to the urologist. He said his private physician was Dr. Jusay, who is a gynecologist, but he didn't know whether Dr. Jusay had sent him. All I could find out that evening was that he had called the emergency room, and, since I was on primary call, they had referred him to me. Why they did not refer him to the urologist on call is a mystery. Oh, well, at least, sleeping on the floor saved the bed.

It Looks Good

In the introduction to this section, I described how some patient interactions are really unusual. This one is not so strange, but the patient obviously did not mean what she said; her mouth got ahead of her brain.

Jancy was working the front desk in our office and was wearing a pretty blouse that she had just bought. As Jane was leaving the office, she saw the blouse and commented on how pretty it was and then blew the encounter when she said, "That blouse looks really good on you. It would look good on anybody!"

Heart Bars

In recent years, it has been found that a high-fiber diet is beneficial in many ways, including good heart and blood-vessel health. This finding prompted one company to develop a high-fiber snack bar they called "Heart Bars." One of the unsettling side effects of a high-fiber diet is an excessive amount of intestinal gas, and the "Heart Bars" had the same effect on some people. My partner, Dr. Wayne Horney, had nicknamed them "Fart Bars" for that very reason, and when I suggested them to Paul for his vascular disease, I told him about this possible reaction. He considered that for a few seconds, and then said, "I can't smell very well, and my hearing is bad, so it won't matter anyway!"

Wait for Sissy

Mrs. Semones was on her death-bed, and the family was gathered around. I was attending her in her last hours, and a number of family members were in the room. She took a deep breath which obviously concerned one of the daughters who cried out, "Oh, mama, don't die until Sissy gets here tomorrow!"

Grape Kool-Aid

I got the following letter from a patient who had been having a strange complaint:

Dear Dr. Booker,

I just had to write and tell you that I found out what is making my stools turn green. I am sure there are other causes, but mine was coming from drinking grape Kool-Aid. I do not know if grape juice would have the same results. Just thought I would pass along this information in case you run into a similar complaint.

Have a nice holiday.
Best Wishes,
Shirley

The Monkeys

Delirium, a noun, from the French *delirare*, de (leave) + lira (furrow) literally means "to leave the furrow (as in plowing)" and is an idiom to say someone "is crazy." Delirium is a mental disturbance marked usually by confusion, disorientation, disordered speech, and hallucinations, although it may be manifest by only hallucinations. It is frequently caused by drugs, both illicit and licit, and the latter was the case with Billy and the monkeys. Billy had hurt his back and was having severe muscle spasms. I was unable to control the pain by oral medications alone, so I put him in the hospital where I gave him a muscle relaxer and a potent intravenous pain killer. The next morning when I made rounds, a nurse casually said, "Watch out for the monkeys in room 415!"

When I walked into Billy's room he looked calm and collected, and there was certainly no evidence of monkeys, even stuffed ones. "Good Morning, Billy," I said.

"Good morning, Doctor," he replied very calmly.

I asked, "What is this about monkeys, Billy?"

He responded in a very controlled, articulate, and reasonable voice, "Doctor, there are monkeys in this room. Nobody can see them but me and, intellectually I know there are no monkeys. Oh, my God, there goes another one up that cabinet! But you can't see him, can you? There are no monkeys in this room. I know it must be this damned medicine, but...oh, lordy, there go two of them behind those drapes; look at that. This damned medicine that's doing this. But, doctor, this is so real, it ain't...." And with this, he ducked his head down and threw up his arms to ward off another hallucinated, but very real, monkey and continued, "...so real, it ain't even funny. They disappear for awhile, and then they are...see? See? They are right back again."

Right away I knew what was happening, and I also knew that as the drugs wore off Billy would be fine, which eventually happened, but it was a lesson for me what drugs and drug interactions can cause in some patients. But it was also hilarious to see Billy reacting to the monkeys he knew were not there!

Here's a Chicken

Ford and Alta were an elderly brother and sister who had never married and lived together on the old family farmstead in a distant part of the county. Ford called me one day because Alta had become ill, and he did not feel he could get her to the office. He asked if I could come out to see her, and I agreed to make a house call later that day.

Now Ford and Alta lived a distinctly agrarian lifestyle, their meager disposable income allowing little in the way of improvements to their home, so I was not surprised at the poor repair of the house. Shutters were askew, broken window panes had been covered with cardboard, and the back screen door was missing the screen wire. Ford herded me down the hall to Alta's bedroom, where I diagnosed her with pneumonia, and told Ford that he could come by the office and get some antibiotic samples, saving them some money. He thanked me profusely as we made out way back down the hall into the kitchen, where I was surprised to see a couple of chickens on the floor, and one perched on the table. It did not seem to bother Ford, as he told me that he couldn't pay me right then, but "maybe this will do until you're better paid." And with that he swiped the chicken off the table by its legs and presented it to me flapping and squawking! I told him that I would just wait until "I was better paid" and beat a hasty retreat to my car while Ford threw the errant chicken out in the yard to live another day.

Turn on the Light

Raymond was an old farmer whom I had taken care of for years. His health was very poor, but he was able to live alone. His wife had died many years before he started coming to see me, and he had never remarried. His children were very solicitous of him, but their pleas for him to come live with them fell on deaf ears. One day as I was finishing up with his visit, he asked me for a prescription for Viagra. Knowing his situation, I was puzzled why, without a wife or girlfriend, he would need Viagra. When I asked him why he needed the Viagra, he rolled his eyes around and, "Well, doctor, I can turn on my own lights!"

This Here Rash

This story came to me years ago by my partner, Walt Barton, whose word is not to be doubted. The story is too strange to be fiction! In those days it was permissible to take garbage directly to the town dump, a function that Walt occasionally performed, and on this Saturday he had made his way to the dump with a load of trash. The custodian of the dump pointed out where Walt could dispose of his trash, and followed him to the indicated site. As the trash was being unloaded he asked Walt if he would take a look at a rash that he had developed. Since the request seemed simple enough, Walt agreed as he tossed the last of the trash in the dump. He turned around to find the man studiously pointing out the offending dermatitis on his penis! Walt related that there he stood in the middle of the town dump, surrounded by trash and squawking scavenging crows, trying to diagnose a penile rash while surreptitiously surveying the landscape to see if anyone else was witness to the last dump-call he ever made!

Gay Sex

And lastly, this story demonstrates the wisdom of not answering too quickly. I had just finished examining Mrs. Atwell, a young woman with a deep southern accent when she asked, "Doctor, can I ask you a question?"

"Surely," I replied.

She asked, "Is gay sex good?"

As I pondered the question and my response, I sought to buy a little time and asked, "Why do you ask?"

She said, "Well, I have been having a lot of trouble with gas recently, and I have heard that Gas Ex is good for that."

I assured her that Gas Ex was indeed a reasonable choice for such a condition, and was really glad that I didn't answer the question I heard!

Poems and Such

Occasionally my patients have waxed poetic, and I include a couple of examples of their creativity as well as one of my own. The following is from one of my now deceased, but favorite patients, Charles Cox, who was a retired school teacher. Charles, always well groomed and with silver hair swept back in a fifties style, was the epitome of debonair. He was erudite and spontaneous, but he surprised me with this literary effort written on June 14, 1993.

The Old Man's Lament

I'm getting older; my life is most spent,
My steps grow shorter, and my back is bent.
My eyesight grows dimmer each passing day,
I have trouble conveying what I want to say.
I arise in the morning and sit on the bed,
Waiting for the faintness to leave my head.
Ever so often, I have a new pain,
So I go to Dr. Booker, and he gives it a name.
I get a prescription for one medicine or more,
And my pill collection rivals that of the store.
Each pill has a time that it must be taken,
And keeping them straight sets my head to aching.
Was it two in the morning? No, I think it was three,
Were they yellow or white? Somebody, help me.
Oh my goodness, my crotch sure is sore,
So off I go to the doctor once more.

My appointment was made to be there at eight,
And I scurry about so I won't be late.
Hurrah! I'm early and sign in on the pad,
The waiting room is full; I think I've been had!
I look at the books and read the interesting stuff,
And for an hour and a half I sit on my duff.
I watch all the others as they come and go,
I think to myself, "That doctor sure is slow."
I won't say it's true, but I have a hunch,
If you sign in at eight, you may get out at lunch.
Hey! They called me! They called me! The nurse has my chart,
She weighs me, takes blood, and checks out my heart.
I pee in a bottle and put it on the shelf,
Then I'm taken to a room to sit by myself.
As I sit there worrying about what's the matter with me,
I hear the doctor laughing with someone in room three.
Then with a smile he enters and sticks out his hand,
"Good to see you, old fellow. How have you been, my man?"
Then the nurse interrupts; it's a call on line two,
Now its ten minutes later, will he ever get through?
He pokes and prods in various places,
And grunts and groans and makes funny faces.
At last he is finished and writes in his book
That he has explored and examined each cranny and nook.
He chuckles loudly as he takes my hand,
"Your briefs are too tight, Charlie, my man."
"Perhaps you should use boxers; they're roomy and loose."
I knew he was thinking, "You silly goose!"
As I left the office, I thought with a smile,
"Ya'll make yourselves comfortable, you'll be here awhile."
Finally, at home, I doctored my head,
Pulled off my clothes and crawled into bed.
I reflected on life, some parts are right nifty,

But somebody lied, it doesn't start at fifty.

Mrs. J was a minister's wife and a very good one, from all I could learn. She was very much involved with the church and was a great help to her husband in his ministerial duties. She came to see me for a physical exam, and I found "a female problem" which I felt required a D & C. She did not feel poorly and was surprised that she needed any surgery at all. Shortly after her visit and the scheduled surgery, she sent me this poem.

No Joke

How about that? I must have an operation!
This thing to me is a strange situation.
I went to the doctor for a routine call,
I had no idea that I could be ill at all!
He found nothing wrong. It must be a trick
Said he must operate to find why I'm not sick.
I wonder what I've got? Is it contagious?
Oh, such a thought is plainly outrageous!
The doctor wore no mask, and I'm not isolated,
I wonder if those precautions are now outdated?
I guess all I can do is wait, worry, and rest.
I wonder if they will give me lots of lab tests?
When they stick in a needle and pull out my blood,
For a full week after, I feel as cruddy as mud.
I hate nurses' white hose! I despise white shoes!
Nurses' white uniforms really give me the blues.
I wonder, exactly, what are the doctor's charge rates,
I guess I should have entered the "Grand Sweepstakes!"
I wonder if this hospital's patients are few,
And the doctor needed something extra to do?
Perhaps the hospital bed should never empty be,

So the doctor filled it up with little old me.
I'll have the operation, and I'll take his nasty old pill,
But the joke is on him, because I can't pay the bill!

The Gemstar was an automated chemical analyzer that we used
for several years before upgrading to a more modern autoanalyzer. It
was a tricky little machine and depended on a special optical lens to
identify the compound. It could run several tests at a time and would
then print out the results with a beeping sound indicating it was printing.
One day our lab techs were befuddled with the failure of the machine
to run the required tests, and they became more and more frustrated
as time went on. Eventually, they discovered that the lens had
developed a dirty film and could not read color changes. Because of
their diligence in solving the problem, I wrote them the following poem.

The Gemstar Saga

It's a crazy machine; they say it has eyes.
They say it talks, but it never cries.
In spite of its eyes, it cannot squint,
But, lo and behold, I've seen it print.
And now they say it has a disease,
It's having trouble with its ABCs.
In spite of its age and education,
It's having difficulty with calculation.
So at last, our Debbie took off its cover,
And looked to see what she could discover.
She pushed and prodded and pulled its springs,
While Sherrl tweaked its diodes and other things.
It screamed for mercy, but they weren't quitters,
They found its eyes and even its printer.
And gazing intently upon its peepers,
They found the problem with the little jeepers.

There in its lenses so round and compact,
The little sucker was growing a cataract!

This next section does not qualify as a poem, so this is the "Such" part of this chapter. This sign appeared on my office door during my first year of military duty in Alaska and it stayed there the entire time. I have carried it with me now for thirty-eight years, and it is time to share it with a wider audience. What prompted the sign, I have no idea, but I liked the idea of my supposed versatility.

Captain Booker

Marriage Counselor
Chief of Wart Clinic
Chief of Psychiatry
(By appointment only)
Chief of Dermatology
(Healer of skin disorders)
Protector of Airmen

Humor Selects

I was at a McDonald's drive-through a while back when the operator suggested that I try an order of "Chicken Selects," the name implying that these particular chicken strips were superior to the regular chicken strips. As I was thinking of a title for this section, it occurred to me that this series of stories is truly "select." They are some of the best stories in my collection.

Go to Hell

This story was told to me by Dr. James Patrickson of Marion, Virginia, a small town west of Wytheville along interstate I-81. Jim is a family physician who was on call in the local emergency room when a female patient of Dr. David Hale's came in with a minor complaint which really did not need emergency-room care. Nevertheless, Jim took care of the problem, and as he was escorting the lady out of the door, he said, "The next time this happens, you don't need to come to the emergency room, you can just go to Hale." Her mouth dropped open, and with a startled expression she turned and, hitting him with her purse, snapped, "Well, you can just go to hell yourself!"

Liquid Assets

An elderly lady who was recovering from a hip fracture was being walked down the hospital hall by Sue, her physical therapist. The lady had a urinary catheter in place, and Sue had the collection bag hooked to her own belt as they slowly made their way down the hall. As I walked by I asked if the lady knew that Sue was carrying her purse.

Without hesitation, Sue replied, "Oh, yes. She asked me to manage her liquid assets."

Miss Carrie

Miss Carrie was 101 years old when she came to live in a local nursing home. Despite her years, she was a spunky old lady, and when I first went in to see her she was complaining vociferously; the floors were cold, the lights were too bright, the drapes were the wrong color, the nurses wouldn't come when she wanted them, the food was not good, etc., etc. I said, "Miss Carrie, you sure are a fussy old woman."

Without hesitation, she snapped back, "How do you think I got to be 101?"

She never stopped fussing and lived to be 106!

Mr. Tom

Tom, a dour little man, was a farmer and a grocer. He was in his eighties when I first met him, and I quickly found that he had a dry wit, which I thoroughly enjoyed. He was originally from Bland County just to the north of us, but had moved to Wythe County as a young man to manage the Piggly Wiggly grocery store and to run his farm. He told me one day that his preacher had come to visit, which was somewhat of an inconvenience, as Tom had farming to attend to. As the visit dragged on and the conversation seemed to have no particular direction, Tom asked him the reason for his coming by. The preacher had noticed that Tom had not been attending services very regularly, and he was concerned about his elderly soul. He finally blurted out, "You, know, Tom, you can't stay here forever. What are you going to do when that day comes?"

Seeking to end the visit, Tom said, "Well, I guess I'll just go back to Bland!" He said the conversation ended shortly thereafter, and he went back to his farming.

Myrtle

Myrtle was a 100-year-old lady at a local nursing home. She had advanced Alzheimer's disease and could not remember more than five minutes in the past, but physically, she was in pretty good shape. She was quite ambulatory, and I would frequently see her sitting at the nurse's desk enjoying the coming and going of the staff and visitors. I took to calling her "Myrt," which she tolerated for a while, but one day she told me, "I never liked 'Myrt,' so call me anything, but that. In fact, "Myrtle" will be just fine." So "Myrtle" it became from then on.

Whenever, I saw her, I would ask her how she was getting along, and she would usually reply, "I'm trying to be okay."

One day when she was all dressed up and looking fine, I told her, "Myrtle, you're looking good. How are you feeling?"

"Well," she replied, "I don't feel as good as I look!" It is obvious that, even with advanced dementia, some of her neural pathways were still open and operating just fine.

A Good Doctor

Dr. Cameron is a bariatric surgeon who has undergone bariatric surgery himself with great success. At one of his lectures on the procedures, I asked him if having had the surgery helped him in his working with patients. He said that it certainly gave him a different perspective and that his viewpoint was generally appreciated by his patients. He said, however, that on one post-operative visit, a patient was complaining of some minor side-effects of the surgery, and he was not very sympathetic, dismissing the complaints with the statement that he himself had undergone the procedure and had no such problems. The fellow replied, "Yeah? Well, you probably had a good doctor!"

Hearing Loss

Mark was being seen for a Department of Transportation physical examination, which requires a hearing test by audiogram. I found him to have a high-frequency hearing loss, which meant that he could not hear high-pitched sounds. I told him that he would not be able to appreciate flute, clarinet, or oboe music in an orchestra and that he would probably not be able to understand some women. He said, "Well, Doc, I don't go to concerts, so that's not a problem. And, you're right, I don't understand women, but it's not because of my hearing!"

Smoking Hell

Mrs. King was a heavy smoker, and I was constantly trying to get her to quit. Teasing her one day, I told her that when she died and got to the pearly gates, St. Peter, having to decide whether he was going to admit her to heaven or send her downstairs, was going to ask her, "How much did you smoke?"

"You know, Doctor," she replied, "smoking won't send you to hell; it just makes you smell like it!"

I Need a...

Anita Anderson was a nurse at our hospital, and one morning, being in a meeting, she was unable to hear the operator paging her on the overhead system. Nevertheless, the operator persisted, "Anita Anderson, Anita Anderson." Finally, one elderly lady called out to the nurse's desk and said, "Would someone please get that lady an Anacin!"

But the story does not end there. Later, Anita remarried and became Anita Hammer. You guessed it; the same scenario "Anita Hammer, Anita Hammer," but this time it was a man who asked his nurse, "I wonder why she needs a hammer?"

You're Number Two

Mrs. Vergie was a very devoted patient of mine who frequently told me that in her life, God was number one, but I was number two. On one occasion, she was to have surgery by Dr. Lee, and as she was going into surgery, she once again, told me, "Now you know, you're number two, and I'm counting on you to get me through this."

I said, "Miss Vergie, since you're getting ready to have surgery by Dr. Lee, don't you think he ought to be number two?"

She thought for a moment and then acknowledged, "Okay, for right now, but when this is over, you go back to number two."

He'll Stay There

As he got older, Bunk developed disabling osteoarthritis, which severely limited his mobility. He was also hardheaded and stubborn, sometimes to the exasperation of this wife, Mattie, and would attempt to do things that she felt he should not be trying to do. She told me one day that she had discovered a way to keep him out of trouble when she was not around. "How is that, Mattie?" I asked.

She said, "I just give him a bath and then leave him in the bathtub, because he can't get out."

Big Problem

My patient, Mr. Smith, suffered from a personality disorder and frequently needed the services of Bill, a counselor with the local mental-health department. For some reason that neither Bill nor I could fathom, Mr. Smith preferred seeing Dr. Moskowitz, a urologist, even for his mental problems. In keeping me updated on the patient's condition, Bill called one day to tell me that Dr. Moskowitz called, and Mr. Smith had just left his office with a flare-up of his disorder. Bill commented wryly, "He must have a deeply-rooted problem."

But Not at the Same Time

Helen had just gotten a new set of dentures of which she was quite proud, because she thought she looked good with them in place. Unfortunately, they did not fit well, and she had to take them out to eat. She told me, "I can look good, and I can eat, but not at the same time."

Fatigue

"Fatigue" is one of the most common complaints heard in family medicine, but no one described it more graphically than Barb when she told me, "I am so tired, my ass is dragging my tracks out." Later, she said that she thought she had developed "anal glaucoma," because "I can't see my ass going to work until I get more energy."

Unusual Remedy

My partner, Dr. Jim Stone, had a patient who also complained of fatigue, but all of the appropriate tests had failed to demonstrate any physical abnormality. Finally Jim gave him a prescription for a multivitamin and told him, "Swallow one of these a day, and don't take a bath for two weeks, and you'll get stronger!"

A Waterproof Shirt

"Honeybear" was a retired United States forester who had spent most of his working life in the wilds of Alaska. When he retired he and his wife returned to their roots in southwest Virginia to live. He was a colorful and rambunctious guy who did not hold with fancy dress, especially coats and ties. One day in the office, he surveyed my rather loud necktie, shook his head, and asked, "Doc, is your shirt waterproof?"

Confused by the question, I said, "I guess not, Honeybear, why?"

He grinned and said, "Because that tie is a real pisser!"

Deaf and Blind

Avis and Bertha were sisters who lived together for years. They were eighty-eight and ninety years old, respectively and were not in the best of health. When Avis told me that Bertha's deafness was getting to be a real problem, I suggested that she write her notes. Avis fixed me with a sharp eye and snapped, "Hell, Doctor, she can't see either!"

Earth

With the advent of hang gliding, there were a couple of fellows in Bland County, just north of Wytheville, who took up the sport, using Big Walker Mountain as their updraft source. Patsy Muncy, a nurse in the intensive-care unit, said that on good days, they could glide for miles before landing in a pasture downwind. One weekend Randy was enjoying a long glide down the mountain, but the wind was dropping, and he decided to set down in a pasture in a remote section of the county. As luck would have it, the wind dropped precipitously just as he landed, and the glider fell on top of him. As he was crawling from under the wing with his goggles and other protective gear on, an old farmer, obviously not familiar with hang gliders, came up to see what was going on. Randy's first question was, "Where am I?"

The old fellow, still puzzling over the strange sight, replied, "On earth."

Memory, Trophies, and Peer Pressure

Bill and his wife, Peggie, moved to Wytheville shortly after their son, Bill, Jr., had moved here as the manager of a local manufacturing company. I was fortunate to have close personal and professional ties with the entire family, and though Bill Sr., and Peggie have passed on, I still have business ties with their grandson, Alan, which date back to Bill, Jr's time in Wytheville.

At age eighty-eight, Bill was not as active as I would have liked, and I advised him to get out more with the people in the retirement center where he lived. He said that was hard for him because most people did not want to hear about what he did twenty years ago, and that was all he could remember!

At age ninety he told me this story about a loving cup. As a young man, Bill had been a competitive sailor and had won many trophies, which he carried with him in his retirement. Over time, Peggie grew tired of cleaning and dusting around them, and gradually they disappeared. Finally, his hoard was down to a single large and elaborate loving cup, which he kept on a shelf in the living room. One morning, while Peggie was out, an old friend from New Jersey called, and he and Bill struck up a lively conversation. The conversation dragged on and on and, Bill's fluid pill began really kicking in. Because he had not talked to this fellow for a long time and was really enjoying talking to him, he didn't want to hang up. Soon he became really desperate and in casting around for a solution, he spied the loving cup. He told me later that he was glad of two things: first, that he had enjoyed sailing so much and second, that he had been good enough to win such a large trophy, because anything smaller would not have sufficed!"

Finally, on his ninety-fifth birthday, I asked him how it felt to be ninety-five years old. He said, "Well, I really don't know, since I've never been this old before, but I can tell you, there's not much peer pressure."

Nobody, but the Undertaker

As Mr. Grimes got older, his health declined, and he began to lose weight. On one visit he told me, "Doc, I've lost so much weight, and tucked up my pants so much, the front pockets are in the back and nobody recognizes me except the undertaker."

Screwed

This next story came straight from the horse's mouth, the horse that had been operated on, herself. Florence and her friend Dorothy were old-maid high-school music teachers, who eventually moved from Virginia to a retirement center in Florida. Both lived into their late nineties, and both were amazingly functional right up until the last few months of their lives. When Dorothy was about ninety-four years old she fell and suffered several fractures of the vertebrae in her neck. The injury was extensive and required a neurosurgeon to fixate the fractures with metal plates and screws to prevent them slipping and causing spinal-cord injury. She recovered without incident, but was perplexed by the neurosurgeon's bland, flat, and unsmiling personality, and she set out to get a smile or a laugh out of him. The opportunity occurred on one of her last visits to him when she inquired of him the exact procedure that he had performed. He explained that the bones were so badly broken that they could not remain in position by themselves and that he had used two specially-designed metal plates, one on either side of the spine and fastened them in place with three screws on each side. Without batting an eye, this ninety-four-year-old lady exclaimed, "Do you mean to tell me that while I was asleep, you screwed me six times?"

The flat, bland was instantly gone as he almost fell off the stool laughing.

Don't Get Us Mixed Up

Smitty Walters is the husband of my lab tech and has been my patient for years. He developed arthritis in his knees and had to undergo arthroscopic examination. He was in the pre-op area with another fellow who was waiting for a procedure as well. Smitty asked him, "What are you here for?"

"I'm going to have a colonoscopy, a prostate ultrasound, a prostate biopsy and a cystoscopy," was the reply.

Smitty thought for a second and said, "Lord, I sure hope they don't get us mixed up!"

Been Overhauled

Mossy had undergone a series of operative procedures, including an appendectomy, a tonsillectomy, an adenoidectomy, a cholecystectomy and a coronary artery by-pass procedure. He and some other fellows were working at their church one afternoon, and even though he was the oldest there, he was doing most of the work. He chided the younger men about his outworking them, but they had the last laugh when one of them retorted, "Well, yeah, but you've had an overhaul!"

I Don't See Well Enough

Miss Annie was an eighty-three-year-old lady who, despite declining health, continued to be very active. She and her neighbor down the block were good friends, and Miss Annie visited her every day, driving her old car around the block and parking in front. I asked her one day why she didn't just walk and get some exercise as well. She replied, "My goodness, doctor, I don't see well enough to walk."

Three Legs

Eleanor had bad osteoarthritis and had to have both knees surgically replaced. She told me that the first operation had gone really well, and she had very little pain with it. Apparently, the second one did not go so well, and she suffered a lot of pain and disability. She told me later, "I'm sure glad I don't have three legs!"

Parents

Ralph was an elderly man who had been under my care for a number of years when I asked him one day if he was staying active. He said that he could not get around too much because of his parents. I was surprised at that, because I knew his parents had passed away years before. He then quickly added, "You know, Mother Nature and Father Time?" I could but chuckle.

Take Two Asprin

The children and grandchildren all called him "Pap," and so did everyone else who knew Mr. Sowers, who owned a plumbing, heating, and air-conditioning business. In the mid 1970s a cold wave plunged southwest Virginia into the minus-twenty range, and Pap regretted his choice of occupations, as he and his men were busy 24/7 with frozen pipes, gummed-up fuel lines, and furnaces that refused to work. It was inconvenient, then, when he developed an abscessed tooth, and called his dentist in the middle of the night to tend to the problem. The dentist, from his comfortable bed, said, "Pap, just take two asprin, and call me in the morning," which Pap did, but not without rancor.

Well, fate has a way of evening scores, and about two weeks later the temperature again dipped below zero, and Pap was awakened in the middle of the night to the desperate voice of the dentist whose furnace had gone on the fritz; "Pap, could you come out and fix this thing, please?"

Although Pap eventually fixed the furnace, he took great pleasure in saying, "Well, Doc, just put two asprin in the tank and call me in the morning!"

Virginia Tech

Wytheville is only about forty miles from Blacksburg, Virginia, which renders me a University of Virginia Wahoo, immersed in a Virginia Tech Hokie environment. Thank goodness, three of us in the medical practice are UVa guys, but that serves as only marginal respite, and I am constantly besieged by one Hokie or another. The ultimate Hokie statement came from Linda, an avid Tech fan, when I was doing a pelvic examination. When I went into the room, she was in the stirrups and draped in the usual modest way with the sheet over her legs and feet. My nurse was snickering, but I thought it was a private joke between Linda and her, so I paid no attention. I sat down at the end of the table, decorously lifted back the sheet and there on the bottom of her right foot was "Va" and on the left "Tech." I nearly fell off the stool laughing and had to leave the room for a few minutes to gather my wits. When I returned, I carried a black magic marker and proceeded to put a "U" in front of the "Va" and scratch out the "Tech!"

He, who laughs last, laughs longest!

A Dual Ceremony

Brenda, one of my receptionists, and her husband sold a few acres of land, including a beautiful little pond, to a local religious group that planned to build a new church on the property. As she was telling our newest partner about the deal, he commented that it was certainly convenient to have a baptismal site right next to the church. Brenda, said, "You sure wouldn't want to be baptized in that pond if you saw the size of the snapping turtles in there."

Our partner, Dr. Rick Grube replied, "Hey, cool! Baptism and circumcision at the same time." It took awhile for all of us to stop laughing.

The Glass Method

Roger is a general contractor who has been my patient for many years. Years ago, during an economic slowdown, we were commiserating about the difficulty of collecting bills when he said that it was too bad that we could not apply the glass method of collection to each situation. Knowing he had left me, he told me about Brownie, another contractor who had called him one day about helping him with a job in another town building a fireplace and chimney onto an already-built house.

Brownie said that the people had a tarnished credit reputation, but times were slow, and the job promised good pay if they could collect. Roger agreed to help him, and they drove to the site, and agreed to build the fireplace and chimney according to the wishes of the couple while they were away on vacation. The job went apace, and as they neared the top of the chimney, Roger went to the local hardware store, and bought a piece of glass that was just a little larger than the hole in the chimney. They laid the glass on the inside edges of the bricks and finished off the last few layers of bricks.

Brownie sent the couple a bill, and shortly received a letter from the wife stating that they were not happy with the job; the bricks were the wrong color and texture, the fireplace design was wrong, the hearth was not centered, etc., etc. Rather than contest the issue in court, Brownie relied on the glass method to get his money. With the first cold snap, Brownie got a frantic call from the husband, saying that when he lit the fire in the fireplace, the house filled up with smoke because the chimney would not "draw" the smoke up. Brownie asked him if he had looked up the chimney to be sure there were no obstructions such as bird's nests, and the man assured him that the chimney was "clear all the way up." Brownie told the man that he thought the problem could be easily remedied, but reminded him that he and Roger had not been paid, and there would be an additional $200.00 for the delinquent payment, interest, and the trouble of returning to the job-site in a distant town. The man agreed to pay the bill, plus the additional charges, and Brownie and Roger drove back to the house. The man met them at the door with a check for the correct amount, and as Brownie started to pocket the check, he detected a hint of triumph in the man's eyes. He handed the check back, and said that this payment had to be cash on the barrelhead. With much huffing and puffing and obvious reluctance, the man went to the bank, and returned with the cash payment, at which time Brownie went inside and laid up a new fire while Roger went up on the roof, and with a large sledge hammer tied to a rope, broke out the glass. Brownie lit the fire and, as expected, the chimney "drew" just fine. Without another word, Brownie and Roger drove back home, satisfied with the success of the glass method of collection.

Many times since I heard that story, I have wished for a comparable glass method of collection for my medical bills. Alas, there is none.

The Birds

Because of the lack of psychiatrists in rural areas, we primary-care doctors wind up taking care of mental illnesses that, in more populous areas, would be the bailiwick of the psychiatrist. John was schizophrenic, but fell under my care when he moved to Wythe County. He had been stable for some time, but came to see me one day because of increasing hallucinations, primarily hearing voices in his head, not a good thing in a paranoid schizophrenic. I felt that he could safely be treated on an outpatient basis, made some alterations in his medications, and had him return in several days. When he came back, he said that he was much better, but was worried because now he was hearing birds talking to him. I made a few more adjustments, and had him come back in a week. At this time, he said that he was back to normal.

"So," I said, "you're not hearing birds talking to you now?"

He regarded me seriously, and said, "Oh, yeah, they're still talking to me," and then he grinned real big and added, "but now I can tell they're lying!"

The alterations we made during "the birds" have kept John on an even keel now for about two years.

A Thoroughbred

James came to see me after his heart attack occasioned by a lax lifestyle. We talked about his rehabilitation program, and I stressed the cardinals of diet, weight loss, and exercise. I told him I wanted him to aim for walking two miles in under thirty minutes. He later told me that the exercise program was really unrealistic, as I was "trying to make a race horse out of a jackass!"

Children

Gassy Norman

Children have provided a few good stories, like this one from my patient, Norman, who was a precocious second grader and whose story came to me by way of another patient who was a guidance counselor at the school. Apparently, Norman had been eating little cinnamon hearts when he thought one had gotten hung in his throat. The classroom teacher referred him to the guidance counselor who would have more time to deal with him. The counselor gave him some orange juice and sent him back to the classroom.

Very shortly, however, he returned to the counselor and said, "Mrs. Lane, it's still in there," whereupon she gave him some water to drink. He stood there for a minute or two testing his swallowing and said, "You know, I think it's still in there."

Trying to use some logic, Mrs. Lane said, "Norman, do you know what happens if you drop a cinnamon heart into a glass of water?"

"Yes, ma'am, it dissolves," he said.

"Well, Norman, that heart probably dissolved a long time ago, and you just have some irritation from where it was lying in your throat."

"Yes, ma'am, it must be gone and I just have some irritation now."

He stood there for a few seconds still testing his swallowing and then said, "Mrs. Lane, I think I would feel better if I burped."

She gave him permission to try that, and after a few forced burps, he said, "Mrs. Lane, I think I'd really feel better if I farted."

Reluctantly, Mrs. Lane granted that permission as well, and after a couple of horrendous passes, he exclaimed, "Gosh, Mrs. Lane, I'm so gassy, I could wilt my desk!"

The story ends there, but I never see Norman, now grown to be a teenager, that I don't visualize his desk wilting under a barrage of odiferous hydrogen sulfide gas!

See Attle

This story came to me by way of my nurse, Robin Dalton, whose young son Seth was about four years old at the time. We had had a rainy spell in Wytheville, and it seemed that the rain would never stop. One day, Robin, in exasperation, said, "It's been raining so long we might as well go to Seattle." Seth thought about this for a few seconds and then asked, "Mom, who's Attle?"

Calm Down, Jesus

Another Dalton rainy-day story occurred when three-year-old Rileigh was leaving a basketball game to go stay with her grandmother. It was raining, and as she and her dad proceeded across the parking lot to their truck, the rain got harder and harder. Finally, Rileigh stopped, looked up into the rain and said in a huff, "Calm down, Jesus; we're just trying to get to the truck!"

A Different Interpretation

The same Rileigh was with her parents watching her older brother play baseball. She was not much interested in the game and was constantly getting out of her little folding chair and running hither and thither. Robin repeatedly put her back in the chair with admonitions to "stay put." After getting out of the chair one last time and almost getting hit by the ball, Robin took her by the shoulders, put her forcefully back in the chair, and said, "You sit right there, and don't get out of that chair again. If your little butt comes out of that chair one more time, we are going straight home." With that, Robin returned to her seat, but could not understand the laughter that followed almost immediately. On turning around, she saw the object of the hilarity: Rileigh streaking down the sideline holding the chair tightly to her "little butt" with no thoughts of giving up her freedom or going straight home!

Who's Riteback?

I was seeing Eleanor for an office visit, and she had her little grandson with her. As I was leaving the room to get her some prescriptions, I said, "Eleanor, I'll be aright back."

As I walked down the hall, I heard the little fellow say, "Granny, what's a riteback?"

Relax

Jeremy was a four-year-old boy who had cut his knee and was in the office to have the wound sewed up. He was anxious, and I told him to relax.

He asked, "How do you relax?" which left me floundering for an explanation understandable to a four-year-old.

I have forgotten what I came up with, but it must have satisfied him as he was good as gold being stitched up. In about ten days, he was back in the office to have the stitches removed. Again, he was a little nervous, and as I was just sitting down with my scissors, he said, "Dr. Booker, tell me how to relax again!"

Until It Frosts

Che was a young fellow when his mother brought him to the office one fall day for seasonal allergies. I have found that the most efficient way to deal with this condition is to use an injection of a long-acting steroid whose effect lasts until cold weather and heavy frost kills off the offending vegetation. As I finished up with Che and his mother, I said, "Well, that will last until it frosts."

As I heard later from his mother, she noticed that he kept looking at the injection site and feeling it every now and then. When she asked him why he was so intent on the area, he said, "I'm just looking to see if it's frosted yet!"

Mama Has Exploded!

Judy was working in her mountain cabin when she fell and hit her chest. She realized that she would probably have a big bruise and looked in the refrigerator for some ice, but none was to be had. The closest alternative was a bunch of ice cream sandwiches which she stuffed into her bra and went on working. Later, when her girls came in, she showed them the area, which by now was covered with melted ice cream sandwiches. Kathy took one look at the mess and exclaimed, "Oh, my gosh, Mama has pigged out on ice sandwiches, and she's exploded!"

Jesus and Barney

Bob's grandson, Seth, had been to his pediatrician for a check up. Since *Barney and his Friends* was a big hit on television at the time, when the doctor started listening to Seth's heart, he said, "Seth, let's see if Barney is in your heart,' whereupon, Seth replied, "Oh, no; Jesus is in my heart; Barney is on my underpants!"

That Won't Work

Before the advent of alternative ways of recording body temperatures, such as ear probes, we relied on oral temperatures to give us the most accurate readings. It is possible to take temperatures under the arm, and these equate to oral temperatures if you add two degrees. A number of years ago, Jared was a youngster who had come to see me because of a cold. His nose was so stuffy he could not breathe when he had the thermometer in his mouth, so Mary Ann, my nurse at the time, tried to take it under his arm. He demurred, saying, "That won't work. I took a shower and put on deodorant this morning, and that will confuse the thing!"

I Can't Read Yet

Eleanor's niece was five years old and was supposed to start school in the fall. She told Eleanor, "I'm going to start school next week, and I can't even read or write. What am I going to do?"

The Fuzz

Little Mark was being seen for a well-child physical. I was asking his mom about his appetite and his diet. She said that he was a good eater and liked most all foods that she gave him. She then paused and said, "It's strange, but we have to watch him pretty close or he will even eat the fuzz off his blanket!"

Fluid Levels

Martha took her eight-year-old son along when she visited her obstetrician for a prenatal checkup with her second child. Her previous pregnancy had been complicated by a deficiency of amniotic fluid, and, after the ultrasound exam, the doctor reassured Martha that she had adequate amniotic fluid in this pregnancy. When they got home from the visit, Landon told his father, "Good news, Daddy, Mommie's got plenty of hydraulic fluid this time!"

Middle of the Road

Davis' little girl was six years old when she asked him, "Daddy, are you old?"

"No," he replied, "I'm young."

"No, you're not," she said. "If you were young, you would be in school like me."

"Well, maybe I'm middle of the road," he said.

Her reply broke him up. "You mean, like a dead possum?"

Ring Knight

When his uncle was to be married, Thor was elected to present the rings to the minister, but he protested vigorously. It turned out that he did not like the idea of being a "ring bear." And so he became the "ring knight," and all went off without a hitch.

The Talking Wall

My pediatric training came from the Children's Hospital of the King's Daughters in Norfolk, Virginia. One day Petey, a four-year-old fellow with pneumonia, was admitted to our service from the emergency room. After he had gotten settled in, his mother asked if she could go home to get him some toys and pajamas. The nurses assured her that Petey would be fine, and that they would look out for him. In her absence, the nurses checked on him frequently, and the ward secretary entertained him over the intercom located over the head of the bed. At first, Petey was confused by the speaker, but he soon caught on, and he and the secretary commenced a lively conversation. His mother returned after an hour or so and checked in at the nurse's desk to find that Petey had, indeed, done very well in her absence. She and the nurse walked into the room, and mom said, "Well, Petey, what have you been doing while I was gone?"

Petey replied, "Oh, nothing much. I've just been talking to that nice wall over there."

Personalities

Much of the material I have collected has been spontaneous and off the cuff, but although the saying was memorable, it did not strike me as particularly characteristic of that person. Some of the stories, however, have stuck with me more because of the people themselves: in other words, the story seemed to be a reflection of that individual's personality. Hopefully, the following stories will give the reader a feel for the storyteller's personality.

Harold

Harold was a stone former and a very efficient one at that. Shortly before his death he told me that he had passed forty-seven kidney stones and, ironically, he died by drowning in an old, flooded stone quarry! Kidney stones are not painful until they fall from the kidney into the ureter, the tube leading from the kidney to the bladder, and then the pain really begins. Small stones may pass with little pain, and, since most of Harold's stones were small, he was able to pass them at home, usually with the help of Dr. Daniels. Dr. Jack Daniels, that is. Occasionally, however, a large stone would lodge in the ureter, and he would be unable to pass it without the intervention of someone with greater expertise than that afforded by Dr. Daniels.

This was the case one New Year's Eve when our senior partner, Dr. Walter Barton, was on call. The office had been relatively quiet, and Walt was hoping that he would be able to get through our New Year's Eve party without being called out. Unfortunately, fate had other plans, as a sizeable stone lodged in one of Harold's ureters. His usual recourse was of no benefit, and he wound up in the emergency room, writhing in pain and more looped than usual because he had begun enjoying the holiday a few hours before the stone hit. Walt was called and arrived in a minor snit, having had to leave the party and his wife, Frances, so precipitously. Minor turned to major when he walked into the alcohol-fumed room and found poor Harold soused to the gills. Although he carried out his physicianly duties rapidly and efficiently, he lost no opportunity to snipe at Harold over his inebriation and every opening resulted in a thinly-veiled insult or dig. This had been going on for a half hour or so when Harold finally said, "Dr. Barton, I know you don't like drunks, and I'm drunk as a skunk, but I'm sick as hell, and you're stuck with me!"

When Walt finally got back to the party, he had regained some of his usual Christian composure and admitted to me that Harold had really brought him back to reality with his exasperated, but hilarious comment. Walt looked a little chagrined, but then with a sly grin, he said to me, "I admitted him to your service!"

Joe

In contrast to many of the other folks I have written about here, Joe, a retired high-school and college teacher is still very much alive. He is a patient and a good friend, who never loses an opportunity to tell me a funny story or kid me about something. When a well-endowed and show-it-off female physician appeared in a local newspaper dressed all in leather and posed sexily on the hood of a Corvette, Joe sent me the article with a note saying that he appreciated all of my prior care, but that he had found another physician who offered something that I couldn't and wanted to transfer his medical records!

Likewise, he sent me the following letter from a patient to Dr. Gott, the author of the newspaper column *To Your Health*.

Dear Dr. Gott:

You doctors are brainwashed by the drug companies. All you ever do is prescribe medications, which only suppress symptoms, not cure disease. There are cures for diseases if you would tell people to go seek alternative medicine. All major diseases can be absolutely cured by homeopathic remedies. Drugs kill people every day; they make people sick. The more drugs you take, the sicker you become. Go study alternative remedies. You will be surprised what you might learn. People need to become aware of alternative medicine and the health care industry. Drugs are the sick care industry.

Attached to the letter was this cryptic note from Joe, "This must be a former patient of yours!"

Other quips from philosopher Joe: "Conscience doesn't stop me from doing anything, it just makes me feel guilty about it," and this one, "Arthritis doesn't stop me from playing golf. I just can't enjoy it."

Joe's father was a very practical fellow and kept young Joe on a short leash. One day his father was upset with something Joe had done and grounded him. Joe took exception and said, "Dad, let's talk about this man to man."

His father replied, "We can't do that, son; we're a man short!"

On another occasion Joe was in the office for a problem that I told him would require a CT scan of the brain. He quipped, "Well, that shouldn't take long."

Our office is right across the road from a large lake, and geese and ducks are constantly on the water. One morning while Joe was in the office the ducks were very noisy, and Joe commented to me that he was glad the quacks were on the lake and not in the office.

And finally, Joe had fractured a rib, which is an extremely painful injury. He was explaining to me that when he had sneezed, "For the first five seconds I thought I was going to die, and for the next thirty seconds I was afraid I wouldn't."

Morris, A.K.A. Joe

As I mentioned in the preface, I have asked most folks if they minded their stories being included in the book. Joe, of the above anecdotes, seemed to be pleased to be included, but then I got the following letter signed by his friend, (and another of my patients), Morris Witten. The letter, which was actually written by Joe, and only signed by Morris, is reproduced below. Once again, I think Joe's personality and his reputation as a "stand-up comic" come out in the writing.

Dr. J. J. Booker, Part-Time Physician
Carilion Family Medicine
1375 West Ridge Road
Wytheville, VA 24382

Dear Dr. Booker,

I have been informed that you are currently writing a book on your experiences as a part-time physician. I also understand that you plan to utilize your relationship with my client, Mr. Joe K. Stanley, as an important chapter. I would advise you to permit him to proofread any and all references about him in your book. I warn you, any disparaging remarks about Mr. Stanley will not be acceptable. If you defame him in any way or cause him any mental or physical stress, I will be forced to take legal action. I am ready and most willing to do so unless we are 100% satisfied with the comments referring to my client. We will not tolerate your taking advantage of Mr. Stanley in the writing of your book. It would be unfortunate for you to antagonize him, because he is your only patient that talks positively about your questionable skills as a doctor. No one else likes you.

Our goal is to acquire at least 50% of the proceeds from your medical practice. When we consider the amount of time you are working, we estimate that we could receive at least $100.00 a year.

I strongly advise you to comply with my request. If you fail to do so, I am coming after you. Remember, let us read or be sued indeed! Failure to do so means that Mr. Stanley will have to look for a **GOOD** doctor.

Sincerely,
M. Witten
Morris Witten, Esq. JD, LLB, MD, VA TECH, UVA, NFL, USA, ACLU, GOP, ERA, PHD, TGIF, WCC, MRI, ACC, NCAA, WPD, FBLA, OBGYN, PETA, LPGA, PGA, DUFFER, PAS, DWI, E&H.

(Author's note: Morris Witten is a retired public educator and, despite the multiple suffixes, has no claim to a law degree!)

They'll Tell You When

Tena has been under my care for years with fibromyalgia, which has been a real burden for her, but she has never lost her sense of humor. Despite having almost constant pain, she is upbeat and joking, and I am always surprised at her resilience. On one occasion she was having difficulty getting her medicine paid for by her insurance company. She was really put out with medical insurance companies in general and spouted out the following tirade, "These insurance companies drive me crazy! They tell you what doctors you can see and when you can see them. They dictate which lab tests and which x-rays you can have and even tell you when you can and can't have them. They tell you what medicine you have to take, even if it's not what the doctor orders. And when you tell them they are playing doctor, they say, 'Oh, no, we aren't; you can have any medicine your doctor orders, we just won't pay for it.' You know, it wouldn't surprise me if next they tell you when you can die, what kind of casket you can have and how deep to plant you!"

And, in retrospect, what she said is about 90% true!

Forty Percent

If ever a story reflects the personality of the teller, it would have to be this one about Edward, a urologist from New York. Ed was overweight, dumpy, and dour, and he tended to look down when he was talking. Early in the formation of the Health Care Financing Administration (HFCA), there were multiple attempts to rein in healthcare costs by cutting physician reimbursement, and some specialists came under more fire than others. After one medical-staff meeting we were talking with Ed about our problems as a result of HFCA's cost-cutting tactics. He stood there shaking his head and then, more animated than I had ever seen him, rendered the following declaration: "You complain? It's perspective you need! Lookit the brain. It's God's temple! You think they cut the neurosurgeons? Never! The neurologists? Never!

"The eye. God's eyes! They never cut the opthalmologists! Never!

"The heart. Source of the soul! Cardiac surgeons? Cardiologists? They got no worry! Nobody messes with the soul!

"The stomach. 'Feed my sheep.' Nobody dares cut the gastroenterologists or the GI surgeons.

"The lungs. Breath of life. They never cut the pulmonologists! The thoracic surgeons? Never! Never!

"The penis. The root of all evil! They cut me 40%."

And with that he shuffled off, leaving us in stitches and realizing that we were not so bad off after all.

Very Proper

The following story is indicative of how personalities alter our perceptions of, and our interactions with each other. This story dates to March 28, 1991, when I was on call in the emergency room. It was a slow night, and several physicians and nurses were gathered in the break room. For some reason, the topic arose of the propriety of nurses calling physicians by their first names. Some of the bolder nurses felt they would not mind at all; others felt that it would not be professional; and still others had mixed thoughts, feeling that it would come down to individual personalities. Fran said that she would not mind calling Dr. Stone and me by our first names, but couldn't imagine herself referring to Dr. Hendrix as "Paul" or to Dr. Stark as "Carl."

Janice agreed and added, "If Dr. Barton and I were naked in the shower together, I would still say, 'Dr. Barton, would you please turn the water on!'"

Don't Be Surprised

In March of 1995, Mrs. Thacker was ninety-two years old and in fairly good health for her years. I had her in the hospital with angina and congestive heart failure. She was aware that her heart was not doing so well, and she told me, "Now, Doctor, don't be at all surprised at what my heart might do, because I had five brothers, and they all died from heart trouble. One of them dropped dead in the bedroom and another dropped dead in the bathroom. One of them had gone to the lawyer's office about his will when he started having chest pain. He drove himself to the hospital at 11:00 A.M. and was dead by 6:00 that night. One was in the dentist's office and started having chest pain at 5:00 in the afternoon and was dead by 10:30 that night. The last brother had a heart attack at home, went to the hospital, but died in a week of pneumonia." Then she added, "And not a one of them was old like me. Jim was eighty-four, Joe was eighty-two, Bill was eighty-eight, Robert was eighty-seven and Paul was only eighty-one!"

Just Tasting

Mattie was a patient of mine when I was a resident physician. She weighed over 400 pounds, and I was constantly trying to get her to lose weight. I talked until I was blue in the face about not eating so much. Interminably, she insisted that she ate only one sandwich and a cup of coffee a day. She was so persuasive that I finally asked her if she would bring one of her children with her on her next visit. I talked to both of them for a few minutes about portion sizes and diet and then turned to the daughter who had come with her.

"Your mom insists that she has only one sandwich and a cup of coffee a day, can you help me understand why she weighs so much, eating so little?"

The daughter rolled her eyes around, looked at Mattie for a few frustrating seconds and then enlightened me with, "Mama's idea of eating is when she fixes only herself something to eat and sits down to eat it, and she's right, she eats lunch by herself, and it is usually a sandwich and a cup of coffee. What she's not telling you is that we have a huge family, and most of us are at home for breakfast, and all of us are there for supper. Mama's reputation as a cook is legendary; she cooks the most wonderful meals you have ever tasted (and here she invited me and my family to a Sunday dinner), and everything has to be just right. Just right comes with her tasting everything a bunch of times with every meal…but to her that's not eating…tasting is not eating…tasting doesn't count…tasting doesn't have calories. Lord, help us, she thinks tasting is not fattening…and look at her…she's the fattest taster in the world."

At last, I had an answer! But it didn't do me any good. Mattie kept on tasting and finally died of blood clots in the lungs, which is not uncommon with folks of that size.

A Drink of Water

Dr. Gruber was a true country doctor in Wythe County, and tales of his exploits abound. This story about him came from another general practitioner, now deceased, Dr. Paul Hendrix. It seems that Dr. Gruber had been called to the scene of a shooting and had attended both the shooter and the shootee. He was later called as a witness for the defendant and testified that the man had been shot in the stomach. The plaintiff's lawyer, in trying to discredit his testimony, questioned him rather caustically; "Dr. Gruber, you made that diagnosis at the scene of the shooting, did you not?"

"Yes, sir, I did."

"I understand that such an injury is difficult to diagnose, and even in medical centers with trained surgeons and radiologists using sophisticated equipment, it may take hours to come to that conclusion. Can you tell the court how a simple country doctor such as yourself arrived at that diagnosis so quickly?"

"I certainly can. I gave him a drink of water, and it ran out of the hole!"

The medically unsophisticated lawyer, stunned by this simplistic answer, had no immediate response, and stammered, "No further questions, Your Honor," and sat down amid the laughter from the jury.

Alice

Although this story has its origins in my internship at Norfolk General Hospital, I include it this section because it so well illustrates the personality of Alice, the night nurse in the emergency room.

In today's training centers, the practice would be frowned upon, but in 1968 it was not uncommon for interns in the emergency room to work shifts of twenty-four hours on duty and twenty-four hours off duty. This was because, opined the graybeards, "It prepared young physicians to become accustomed to long hours and unpredictable situations while attending the sick and injured." In reality, it made staffing the emergency room a great deal easier for the hospital administration! At any rate, I began my internship year in the emergency room, not looking forward to the grueling work schedule. The last eight hours of the shift, from 11:00 P.M. to 7:00 A.M., were especially tough, not only because of fatigue, but because circadian rhythm had an affect on all of us, even those just coming to work in the middle of the night, when normal people were sleeping. The one exception was Alice, RN. Alice was a retired United States Navy nurse who was working on her second career as an emergency-room nurse, and if there was ever personification of a "fireball," Alice was it. When she arrived things started happening; patient flow increased, delinquent paperwork got finished, supplies got restocked, backlogged lab and x-ray reports suddenly appeared on the charts, and the energy level of the entire department shifted upward. Her philosophy was that it was easier to pull a chain than it was to push it, and her management style was to lead by example. If, for example, the janitorial staff was slow getting a room cleaned and prepared for another patient, it was not beneath Alice to grab a mop and bucket and do it herself. It soon became apparent that everyone in the department was more diligent, as they did not want to have a reputation for Alice doing their jobs!

We interns loved Alice, not only because she made things hum, but because she loved us and cared for us like a mother hen. If we had missed supper, it suddenly appeared; if our uniforms were soiled, clean ones were made available; if misplaced charts were holding us up, they were miraculously found, and if we were behind because a specialist had not responded to our request, he or she just happened to drop by.

Alice was nothing if not efficient, but she will be forever remembered by us beleaguered young physicians because she recognized our limits and aided and abetted our respite. Before nurse practitioners and before physician's assistants, there was Alice, and because of her navy training, she was skilled at many of the tasks that we interns were responsible for. It did not take long for me to recognize her merit when on one shift we had been swamped with numerous critically-ill and injured patients, and I had been just hammered. I had been on the go constantly since 7:00 A.M., stressed with medical decision making, gone without lunch or supper, and was just exhausted as the department finally cleared out about 2:00 A.M. Alice took me by the hand, and led me to a seldom-used room, wherein I found a cot made up with sheets and a blanket. "Get in," she said. "I'll call you if anyone needs you." I passed into a dreamless sleep until I awoke to Alice coming into the room at 7:30 A.M.! No patients for five and a half hours? Come on, now! Some sort of record! Unheard of! Impossible!

Nothing of the sort. Alice sat down on the bed and gave me a handful of charts to review and sign, indicating that I had approved all of the treatment. As I read over each excellently documented chart, it was evident that Alice had substituted for me in an amazingly efficient way. The minor colds, headaches, sore throats, bumps and bruises, and even the minor lacerations had been handled as well or better than I, as a brand-new physician, could have done. I signed off on all of the charts, kissed Alice on the cheek, and went home to my wife, who was amazed that I did not, as usual, collapse in my recliner and sleep for the rest of the day.

The remainder of my rotation in the emergency room was marked by an easy association between Alice and me, and in addition to making my life much easier, Alice showed me how a positive, upbeat attitude makes life easier for everyone. I hope that, over the years, I have been able to influence other people in the same way Alice influenced a new, wet-behind-the-ears physician who, many times, did not know as much as his nurse!

Shucks

Since my wife and I were both raised in farming communities, we wanted our children to have the same experience, and after a few years in Wytheville, we bought a farm and began raising purebred Dorset sheep. Staples of their diet were alfalfa and corn, both of which we raised on the farm. One day we were picking corn when a patient stopped by to ask about some lab tests that he had gotten (office calls, house calls, barn calls, field calls, etc., were not uncommon). As we were talking, he idly started pulling off ears of corn, shucking them, pulling off the silks and tossing them into the wagon hooked to the corn picker. After a minute or so, he said, "I'll bet you a Coke that I can pull off the ears, shuck them, pull off the silks and put them on the ground faster than you can pick them up and throw them in the wagon." Having watched him do the picking, shucking, and silking, I figured that I could pick up the ears and toss them in the wagon much quicker than that, so I said, "You're on!" I watched as he casually walked over to the next stalk, picked off an ear, shucked it, and pulled off the silk, but I was not prepared when he reared back and tossed the completed ear fifty feet to the left! Needless to say, the next ones went everywhere except on the ground at our feet! It did not take me long to realize that I had been bamboozled by an old country gag. Having learned the valuable lesson of not betting a man at his own game, I later bought him his Coke at the local gathering place.

Love Springs Eternal

We tend to relegate older people to the heap of uninteresting and unexciting personalities, but Miss Jean defied that stereotype. She was the most elegant and attractive ninety-year-old woman I have ever met. She was tall and slim, immaculately dressed, and sharp as a tack. Even with all of these attributes, I was surprised when she told me that she was getting married. "Gosh, Miss Jean," I exclaimed, "that's really nice. Have you known this fellow very long?"

"Oh, just a few years," she replied. "We were in the first grade together!"

To paraphrase, love springs eternal from the human breast.

I Don't Need the Cadillac

Jim was nearing seventy when he needed a total knee replacement. During his pre-operative evaluation, he asked the orthopedist how long the prosthesis would last. When he was told that it should last over thirty years, he said, "Well, at my age, I think the fifteen-year model should do me just fine!"

Situations

Most of the stories in this book take their humor from anecdotes, quips, one-liners or punch lines, but there is much humor to be found in situations themselves with little or anything being said. This next series of stories has very little in the way of conversations, but it is the uniqueness of the circumstance that makes them funny.

A Case of Seizures

Once again, I am indebted to Dr. Jim Stone for this story. He had a patient, I'll call Susan, who had a long history of "seizures." She had seen many physicians and had many medical evaluations, none of which ever showed any evidence of physical disease, and the spells were attributed to hysteria, a type of psychological reaction to stress. Her husband had grown used to the spells, since, even though they might last as long as an hour or so, they never resulted in any adverse outcomes. One cold and blustery February night Susan was having a series of such "seizures" and was brought to the emergency room where Jim was on call. Now Jim is a thorough history taker, and in talking to the husband, he discovered that the patient had upper and lower dentures, and was very vain about wearing them all the time. Her husband related that one time when she was having such a spell, he tried to remove the dentures and the jerking stopped.

Sensing the dawn of enlightenment, Jim left the husband in the waiting room, and called two nurses to the doctor's station where he told them that if Susan should begin another "seizure, they were both to go into the room, and one say to the other, "If she doesn't stop soon, we'll have to take out her dentures to keep her from swallowing them." Sure enough, it was not long before Susan began having another "seizure," and the two nurses carried out their theatrics perfectly. The "seizure" stopped abruptly! From then on, just the mention by anyone of removing her dentures stopped Susan's spells immediately.

Later, with the condition having been defined as psychological, intense counseling resolved her underlying problems and the "denture therapy" was no longer necessary.

Pointers and Setters

Dr. Wayne Horney was the fourth physician to join our practice and is an avid hunter. Over the years he has accumulated numerous trophy deer, elk, and caribou heads, full-sized stuffed wild turkeys, multiple wild turkey tail feathers and beards and other memorabilia of his hunting exploits. Since his wife would not allow him to bring them home, he had them hanging all over the walls in his office and the adjacent hallways. Because of his hunting prowess, we accorded him respect that he should know his hunting dogs, although this story involving pointers and setters is not about dogs.

One afternoon he discovered a very wet spot in one of his examining rooms. A thorough search for a leaky roof or water pipe led to naught, and he began to suspect some other etiology for the dampness. He went to the lab and returned with a urine dipstick and further testing revealed the effluent to be consistent with urine. As our nurses went through the list of patients seen in that room in the afternoon, they came up with three male suspects. I saw that several females had also been in the room as well and asked why they were not included in the suspect list? Wayne then pointed out that the wetness was in the very corner of the room, and the act obviously had to be the work of "a pointer and not a setter!"

He's Right Here

This story comes from Patsy Muncy, a registered nurse who has supplied me with a number of funny stories over the years. In this one, she was working on the medical floor and on night rounds they could not find an elderly male patient. He was very small and had Alzheimer's disease, and the staff was concerned that he had wandered out of the hospital. A frantic and thorough search of all the rooms, closets, toilets, visiting areas, classrooms, and elevators failed to locate him. As the nurses congregated in the hall outside of his room, the man in the room across the hall asked what was going on. Since he was also somewhat demented, the nurses tried to explain in simple terms that they were concerned about Mr. Crockett's disappearance.

At that, the man said, "Well, he's right here."

The nurses looked all around and saw no one at all. Puzzled, they asked, "Where?"

"Right here," he said, and flipped back the covers on the bed to reveal the little fellow all curled up at the bottom of the bed fast asleep!

Ice Cream

At one time, Wythe County Community Hospital patients were given the opportunity to recognize and reward individual nurses for their special attention to the patient. This was done through "Reward Cards" filled out with the nurse's name and signed by the patient. The reward was a big dish of ice cream in the cafeteria. The nurses all enjoyed this, but became puzzled that several nurses kept getting multiple ice cream rewards, even from patients that they were not taking care of. The initial thought that they were filling out the cards themselves was quickly dismissed, and the staff surreptitiously went into sleuth mode to discover the culprit.

Gene had been in the intensive care unit with a serious heart attack. He had grown fond of his ICU nurses who, he said, had saved his life. As he got better, he was transferred to the general medical floor to finish his recuperation. Since he was quite ambulatory by that time, he wandered the halls freely at all times of the day and night and was accepted by the staff as "rehabilitating." On one such sojourn, he apparently discovered that the reward cards were kept on the housekeeping carts, and he began to swipe them, fill in his favorite nurses' names and forge other patient's signatures on the cards! The mystery of the nurses' sudden weight gain had been solved.

Not One Skinny Dime

Mr. Rankin was an Alzheimer's-disease patient in a local nursing home for several years before his death. He had very little physical disease, was ambulatory, and was easy to care for. As some demented patients are wont to do, he had an invariable routine each morning about 7:00 just before breakfast was served. He would walk slowly down the hall to the nurse's desk, lean over the desk to peer at the nurse on duty and say, "Well, I've been working here for twenty years, and nobody has paid me one skinny dime, and I'm not going to stand for it anymore!" With that, he would shuffle back down the hall to his room and eat breakfast.

Professional Wrestler

Warren was a nineteen-year-old male who had come to my office for a pre-employment physical exam. He was a strapping, muscular young man who looked like he could take on the world and score points. The physical exam was normal, as was the lab work. The surprise came when I told him the job required a tetanus shot. "Oh, no, you're not giving me one of those!" he exclaimed. "Those things hurt! I can't stand that. Please don't give me a shot." The job he was applying for? A professional wrestler.

Betsy Marie

I have two patients who are sisters. They were born about a year apart, and apparently their parents had a strange sense of humor as they named them both "Betsy Marie." To avoid further confusion, they called one "Betsy" and the other "Marie," but whenever both were wanted, they would call, "Betsy Marie!"

Hot Sausage Biscuits

Mrs. Copenhaver was a ninety-six-year-old lady in a local nursing home. The nursing staff was puzzled by her frequent requests for a heating pad, since she had never complained of anything for which such an appliance would be used. Nevertheless, she continued to ask for one, and finally her family bought her a really nice unit. Afterwards, the nurses noticed that she never used the pad on her joints or muscles, and she would not say what she was using it for. One Saturday, I was at the home and stopped by to do a routine check on her. As the nurse and I worked through the physical exam, I found the heating pad folded up down by her hip. As I moved it out of the way, a nice warm sausage biscuit fell out! She had been using the heating pad to keep her breakfast sausage biscuits warm for later in the morning!

This Shoe Hurts

Bill, whose tales occupy space elsewhere in this volume, was ninety-four at the time of this one. He had fallen, but had gotten back into bed by himself. When the nurse arrived, he was complaining of pain in his back. He said it felt like a huge knot pushing up into his right upper back and when he moved the pain got worse. As the nurse investigated further, she found that he was lying on his shoe!

I Wonder How

Mr. Dunford was an elderly man in the intensive-care unit with congestive heart failure and much confusion due to poor circulation. He had been a heavy smoker and refused to quit even in the face of his increasing heart and lung disease. As a routine part of ICU monitoring, he had a pulse oximeter on the end of his right forefinger. This is a device that glows bright red and the sensor can "read" the amount of oxygen in the blood. The nurse called me into the room to watch him react to the oximeter. Strangely, he kept putting the knuckle of the right hand in his mouth. After a few seconds, he would take it out and gaze quizzically at the hand. After a few minutes of watching this, I went in the room and asked him what he was doing. The answer almost floored me! He could see the red glow at the end of his finger and thought it was the end of a cigarette he was smoking…he just couldn't figure out how to get it in his mouth without it burning him!

Just Little Old Us

Debbie, our lab tech, called Mr. Hamblin back to get blood drawn, but he had disappeared, and we could not find him anywhere. We decided that he must have gotten tired and left. Later we found Mr. Hamblin in an examining room with Mrs. Anderson, and the two were just having a wonderful time talking and cutting up.

As we pieced the story together later, it seems that Mrs. Anderson had been brought to the office by her husband, who stayed out in the waiting room while she was being examined. After waiting for a while in the examining room, she got lonely and asked the nurse to call her husband back to sit with her. My partner, Walt Barton, had a new nurse who did not know the patients very well, but she called Mr. Anderson over the intercom. Both being hard of hearing, Mr. Anderson did not hear, and Mr. Hamblin thought it was he being called, so he walked on back. Libby put him in the room with Mrs. Anderson, none the wiser for her mistake. Well, when Walt walked into the room a little while later, he was totally confused, knowing both Mrs. Anderson and Mr. Hamblin. Having no earthly idea how they both got into the same room, Walt quickly exited the room and called for Libby to straighten things out. A good nurse is hard to beat in those situations, and things quickly got sorted out with Mr. Anderson in the room and Mr. Hamblin back in the waiting room.

Lew

Pharmaceutical representatives are always looking for ways to make an impression on physicians in such a way that the latter will be inclined to use their drugs. Lew was and is an excellent rep, who is always coming up with gimmicks to give him an edge in the dog-eat-dog world of selling medicines. I do not remember any of Lew's conventional approaches, but two failed details will stick with me forever.

One of his products was a nasal spray called Nasacort AQ, which was supposed to have a special chemical property of coming out of the bottle as a fine liquid, but turning immediately into a gel so that it would stay in the nose and not drip out. For his demonstration, he brought out two wine glasses. He went to the sink and turned one glass upside down, quickly demonstrating that nasal spray A, when sprayed into the glass, just ran out into the sink. Then, grinning like the proverbial Cheshire cat, he stepped back on the carpet and sprayed Nasacort AQ into the second glass. Lo and behold, the Nasascort AQ also dribbled out of the glass and all over the carpet! Poor Lew looked horrified and, as my nurse and I doubled over with laughter, he grabbed a paper towel and began mopping up the mess.

The second of his mishaps involved a drug called Allegra. Although it was a potent antihistamine, Lew said that it did not have sedating properties like other such drugs and would not cause confusion and was so safe, it could be taken in large doses without consequences. One tablet a day was the recommended dose, but to make his point, he went to the sink, drew a glass of water and took three tablets at one time. He made a big point that no other antihistamine was so safe and so free of sedative side-effects that a pharmaceutical representative would dare to take three times the recommended dose. With that, he smugly packed up all of his detailing paraphernalia and walked off down the hall obviously feeling very good about having made such a dramatic appeal for the use of his drug. I called after him, "Hey, Lew, come back, you forgot your computer," which he had left on the counter!

Although, no representative would set out to make an impression in such a way, there will be many who will come and go and I will never remember their names or their drugs, but Lew? I'll never forget Lew and his two medicines…or, for that matter, his two botched details.

How About That!

There is an elderly man in our practice with the unlikely name of Saint Andrew Barker. Interestingly, he lives on St. Peter's Road in Speedwell, Virginia!

It's Snowing!

One February day, I was making early morning rounds at the nursing home when Melanie, the nurse accompanying me, told me she had caught Lester trying to open the blinds "to see the snow" and then Dan had asked her how hard it was snowing. Puzzled that both men thought it was snowing when the weather was clear, she suddenly caught on…both men were watching "The Weather Channel" broadcasting from Chicago!

You Can Have It

This next story came to me from Dr. Davis Moore about his long time partner, Dr. S., both family physicians in Wytheville and both graduates of the University of Virginia School of Medicine (a long time ago). His partner was a quite gadabout in his younger days and drove an Indian motorcycle. One weekend after a round of partying, he was somewhat under the influence and was riding the Indian when he made a wrong turn and crashed into a reflecting pool on campus. He was not hurt, and as he was standing there surveying his situation, a man happened by and inquired if there was anything he could do to help. He said, "No," that he was fine, but asked him if he would like to have a motorcycle. The man said he certainly would, whereupon He climbed out of the pool, and pointing to the Indian, said, "It's all yours" and staggered on home never to ride a motorcycle again!

Sow and Piglets

I spent the summer of my first year in medical school with a veterinarian, James Robert Huntley, in our local town. Without a doubt, this was one of the best experiences of my early training, and it shaped my thoughts about service in a small town and with small town people. I learned about caring for creatures totally dependent on their human masters for their welfare, and I would later use that ability in caring for my many demented and physically-helpless patients in nursing homes. I also honed my surgical skills in his operatory and learned the sometimes tedious nature of post-operative care, which was one of my duties. My skills in our dog lab operations in medical school were far beyond my fellow classmates because of my earlier training, and I was grateful for my unorthodox way of acquiring my abilities. But on to the humor.

I had heard from my grandfather, a farmer, the danger posed by sow hogs when they had piglets. They are extremely protective and will attack anything threatening their babies. He told frightening tales of them "popping" their mouths open so wide that the lower jaw appeared unhinged and then slashing from side to side with their lower tusks to rip and tear into their victims. He also related the story of his son, my uncle, who had been caught in just such circumstances and was badly injured. It was, therefore, with great trepidation that I struck out one early morning with James Robert to vaccinate a litter of piglets. When we arrived at the farm, I was reassured when the farmer told us that he had sequestered the sow in a field separate from the piglets, and we would be able to work without worrying about an attack from Mama. The piglets were in a small enclosure with a small covered shed for us to pen the piglets in for the vaccinations. The farmer helped us to corral the piglets, and he then went off to attend to other chores. James Robert and I laid out our paraphernalia and we alternately caught a piglet while the other gave the vaccination. Then we set the patient outside the pen so it would not get a second shot.

Needless to say, the piglets were not happy away from Mama and, in addition, being injected with a vaccine that hurt. They protested mightily, and amid the noise from them, we did not hear the sow rip through the fence and come charging across the field at us. My first clue was when James Robert yelled, "Run!" I looked where he was pointing and saw the fearsome thing I had been warned about. The sow was running faster than I could have imagined an ungainly animal like that doing. I now understood the term "popping" as she alternately opened and closed the maw that practically hid the rest of the huge animal coming at us like a freight train. I was considerably younger than James Robert and made it to the small shed before he did, then helped him to leg it up on top. We just made it to the top just as the sow arrived with popping, swinging jaws and saliva flying! We felt we were safe until she reared up on her hind legs and was so long she could almost reach us even as we crowded to the opposite side of the roof. For the next ten minutes or so, James Robert and I jumped from one side to the other as the sow circled the building snorting, grunting, popping her jaws, salivating, and, in general terrifying a medical student who wished he had stuck with human subjects!

Eventually, the sow gathered her litter and lay down for them to nurse, and James Robert and I were able to slip off the back side of the pen, and creep out of the field. As we reached the safety of our truck, I reminded James Robert that we had left all of our gear in the pen. He looked at me with a grin and said, "Why don't you go back and get it?" We left it there!

Prepare for Launch

Miss Hallie was eighty-four years old and lived in the old family home. She had an old-fashioned, high, four-poster bed that was difficult for her to get into, and she had to use some special maneuvering to accomplish the feat. She would hike one knee onto the bed and then leap off the floor, launching herself onto the bed on her face and right shoulder. She would then squirm around using the headboard as a fulcrum until she was straight in the bed. One night, the launch was particularly vigorous and carried her off the other side of the bed. It was the next day when she came to the office with a dislocated right shoulder! From then on, she used a stepping stool to make a less athletic approach to the bed.

Hard Headed

Dale was a farmer who came to my office one morning with a swollen and painful right hand. He was very tender over the base of the little finger, and a subsequent x-ray revealed a fracture of the fifth metacarpal, the so-called "boxer's fracture" because it often occurs when hitting an opponent in a crossing swing. I asked Dale how he did it, and he mumbled about "hitting something." I continued working with him, and asked again later how it had happened. Sheepishly, he told me that he had gone out in the morning to check his sheep flock, and found a ewe had delivered a lamb. As he was carrying the lamb to the barn, the ewe kept butting him in the leg. Finally, in exasperation, he tried to head her off by hitting her with his fist. Unfortunately, missing all of the soft wooly parts of her anatomy, he whacked her right in the head! Didn't bother her at all, but it broke his hand!

Big and Little

Miss Vergie's husband worked for the railroad for years, and when he died, she was left with railroad benefits, including health care. She never paid a dime out of pocket for her visits to me, but always brought me a "tip." These tips were originally Liberty or Eisenhower silver dollars, but later she switched to Susan B. Anthony dollars. One day she told me she felt these were "too little" and asked me about what I thought. I told her that I really liked the bigger ones. A mistake! From then on I got Kennedy half-dollars.

I have kept all of Miss Vergie's tips and plan to pass them on to my grandchildren with a copy of this story.

"It's Only a Turkey"

My partner, Dr. Wayne Horney, is an avid and proficient wild turkey hunter, and a myriad of trophies attest to his prowess. Most of these are "fans," the spread tail feathers, mounted on a cushioned board, but two are fully mounted huge gobblers, one standing on the ground and one in flight. The latter, with its wings fully spread, is an impressive sight and was mounted on his office wall as though flying out of the door.

Late one night the police dispatcher called to notify me that the burglar alarm in our office had gone off, and would I open the building for the officers to investigate. When I arrived a few minutes later, the police had already surrounded the building, and I opened the door for them to check the inside. I followed two of them down the hall as they methodically checked each room, one using his flashlight and the other swinging his gun into the room, prepared to accost any intruder. All went smoothly until they reached Wayne's office where they performed their routine, only to catch the monster turkey winging its way right into their faces! "My God," one of them yelled and stumbled back into the second who fell into me. It took only a second or two for them to realize what it was, but I dare say, they were much better prepared for a human intruder than a wild turkey!

Tomato Vines

Dr. Os Finne, a general surgeon in Wytheville in the 1970s, was fond of tomatoes, and at one of our hospital staff meetings, he regaled the doctors at our table about raising tomatoes at his home when he was in surgical training. He had read an article about a method of growing tomatoes that purportedly resulted in such huge crops that only a few plants were necessary to feed even large families. Since he was single at the time, he decided to plant only three vines, and set about putting the system in place. His backyard was rather small, so he decided to put the plants next to the house to save space. The article emphasized that it was the soil/nutrient system that was the key to the process; it started with digging a hole three feet square and three feet deep. The hole was then to be backfilled with very specific and progressive layers of coarse gravel, fine gravel, sand, leaf mulch and finally top soil mixed with cow manure. Specific types and amounts of nutrients were to be added at each level and mixed in well.

Os followed the directions to the letter, and then planted a tomato vine in each hole. It did not take long for them to start growing as he carefully watered and top-dressed the vines with additional fertilizer. The vines soon needed staking, and then the stakes had to be replaced with longer ones. As summer went on, the vines outgrew the stakes and had to be supported by wire cages fastened to the wall of the house. Amazingly, the vines grew over the gutter and proceeded to grow up the sloping roof. Os, awed by the prolific vines, invited family, friends and neighbors to view the project and was rewarded by compliments of what a great gardener he was. When the blossoms appeared, they were indeed multitudinous and the vines looked like "a white cloud" covering the wall and roof of the house; and the compliments kept coming. The mayor came by, and the local newspaper carried an article about the project.

Os was in seventh heaven as he anticipated the late summer harvest and began plans to preserve the crop. He devoured the gardening journals, gleaning tips on canning, juicing, drying, saucing, and other methods of prolonging the culinary delights of his beloved tomatoes. He procured all of the necessary ingredients for the different forms of preserving, along with jars, lids, rings, drying equipment and other appurtenances which he felt needed to be on hand to handle the prodigious task awaiting him.

At this point, Os paused, with everyone hanging on his every word and awaiting the glorious conclusion to the story. He drew a deep breath, and pretended to wipe a tear from his eye as he concluded, "Such beautiful, beautiful vines," he sighed, "and not one damned tomato!"

Apparently, blight had affected all of the blossoms at a critical stage in their development and no tomatoes formed.

Odds and Ends

Which Are You?

Bill went to visit Mr. Aker at his milking barn. As he walked in, he called out "Good morning, Mr. Aker."

Mr. Aker replied, "Only two types of people call me 'mister;' them who don't know me and them who want to borrow money; which are you?"

Not Much Anymore

I had hospitalized Mrs. Dix with pneumonia. Now you must realize that Mrs. Dix was an eighty-nine-year-old lady who weighted only ninety-eight pounds. As I was listening to her chest, she said, "I'm sorry, Doctor, but I can't show you a cleavage anymore."

Just a Mite

Mr. Bevil and I had a common hobby in raising honeybees, and frequently discussed the growing problem of tracheal mites, which were causing a lot of problems in bee colonies in our area. He came to see me once with the complaint of stomach pain, and I discovered that he had become infected with a germ which had caused an ulcer in his small intestine. Giving him some background on the condition, I explained that this organism had been discovered to cause ulcers many years ago by an Australian who named the bug "Campylobacter Jejuni," but teased him saying, "That name was too hard to say so they changed it to 'Helicobacter Pylori.'" He gave me a blank stare, and I knew that I had gone over his head, so I left it that he had developed a "stomach mite" to which he easily related, and we then went about curing the "mite" with a series of antibiotics.

Feeding the Groundhog

Mr. Bevil of the above story lived alone in a house across the road from the post office in Ceres, Virginia, a hamlet in Bland County. He was getting up in years and was somewhat lonely when a new young female post mistress took over running the show. She was friendly and outgoing, and he began visiting the post office frequently during the day. She did not seem to mind his company, as that particular job in Ceres could be monotonous. After a few weeks, a number of inhabitants of the community began to notice a very distinct path being worn between his house and the post office and teased him about "his affair" with the young lady. He wasn't about to stop his visits, so he began carrying a carrot with him to the visits. When next someone commented on the path, he told them, "I'm going over there to feed that groundhog what lives under that there shed next to the post office." And that was the end of that!

Colors of Pain

These days, a lot of attention is paid to the degree of a patient's pain. Nurses constantly evaluate pain, with the idea that significant pain is unacceptable, as we have multiple ways to alleviate the discomfort. Typically, the patient is asked to rate the pain on a scale of one to ten where one is the mildest pain, and ten is the worst pain imaginable. In January of 1990, Mrs. Holley had devised her own scale of pain, and it was nothing I had ever encountered before...she graded pain by color with the worst being red, and the least being green. Grey and yellow were intermediate grades of pain! I never did learn the system completely, but when she had a heart attack, I knew that her red chest pain was bad, but the grey arm pain was not as bad and the green pain in her back was not bad at all. Though this mode of communication was confusing to others, Mrs. Holley and I got along just fine with it, and I was able to alleviate her pain very effectively.

As I have thought back on this episode over the years, it has occurred to me more than once that "communication" is the ability to understand each other regardless of the terms used. Sometimes patients use unusual ways of expressing themselves, and the astute physician must be constantly alert to those unfamiliar ways of communicating or we miss vital clues that would otherwise help us to treat the problems. As the famous French physician, Laennec, said, "Listen to the patient; he will give you the diagnosis."

They Dress a Fellow Up

This story was told to me by Dr. Susan Mourot, another family physician in Wytheville. Before newer therapies for prostate cancer were available, an alternative treatment was to eliminate testosterone, the male hormone that fosters the growth of the cancer, by removing the testicles. Susan had a ninety-three-year-old male with prostate cancer, and this treatment was recommended. He refused and Susan, trying to convince him to change his mind, pointed out that he was ninety-three and his wife was eighty-six, and the appendages certainly were of little use to him. His reply contained a grain of truth, but left her in stitches when he said, "Yes, ma'am, I knows that, but I'd like to keep 'em; they kind of dress up a fellow."

They Liked to Killed Him

Stella was a backwoods woman in the far reaches of mountainous Bland County. She had a plethora of children, and Rhonda, the public health nurse, discussed birth-control pills as a means of limiting the family size. Stella seemed to be amenable to this approach, but a few months later she came to the health department, pregnant once again. When Rhonda expressed surprise that the pills had not worked, Stella said, "Oh, Lord, Miss Rhonda, them things liked to kill poor old Charlie. He 'bout puked his guts out, and he quit taking them."

Rhonda told me later that Stella knew the pills were "usually" taken by the wife, but she figured that since she couldn't get pregnant without Charlie, he was the one to blame and he ought to be the one to take the pills!

A Foreign Language

Harry loved to tease, and never wasted an opportunity to josh me. One day in the office he asked me, "Why is it that when a doctor starts examining you, he starts talking in a foreign language?" I was at a loss as to where he was going with this, so I played along. "What do you mean, Harry," I asked. "Well, you know, I went to get my eyes checked by Dr. Kiser, and as soon as he started looking my eyes, he began saying, 'hmm, un huh, hmm, huh, ooo, huh, hmm,' and I couldn't understand a word he said!"

Went out on My Wife

Wayne was the sort of fellow who tended to beat around the bush when telling me his problems, and his stuttering did not help me to understand much better. He came to see me about his heart disease and allowed that he was afraid that he was going to die. He said, "Doc, I've got to clean up my act. I'm eating better and walking a mile every day. I've done quit cussing, and I'm going to church regular, but I still went out on my wife for the first time last week." He paused and then said, "You know, it didn't feel like I thought it would. It did make me weak and dizzy, but I wasn't short of breath, and I didn't have any chest pain, so I thought I was all right after it was over."

He paused, and as I sought to clarify this situation, I said, "Well, Wayne, since you're doing so well with cleaning up your act, what possessed you to do that?"

He shook his head and said, "Gosh, Doc, I don't know; we were just standing there, and the next thing I knew I woke up on the floor. I just went out like a light!" At that point, I went out…out of the room, where I could laugh without compromising our doctor-patient relationship. Wayne has remained a patient for many years, and as far as I know he has never gone out on his wife again.

Needling Her

Mr. Rash and his wife were patients of mine for years, though both are dead now. His wife had severe osteoporosis, and at that time, one of the few therapies was a medicine called Calcimar. It could only be given intramuscularly, and I taught Timble how to give the shots. After a month or so, I saw them back in the office and asked him how he liked giving her the injections. "Well, Doc," he said, "I really enjoy needling her since she's needled me for so long."

An Eighty-Year-Old Woman

Mrs.Hanshew was an eighty-year old lady with a number of medical problems, including lung disease, heart disease, arthritis, and osteoporosis, to name a few. She was in the hospital when I went by to see her and asked how she was feeling. She said, "I've got more aches and pains than..." and she paused while she gave this some thought and added, "than an eighty-year-old woman!"

A Hair Cut

Even lab couriers have contributed to this tome. Sam was responsible for picking up our lab specimens twice a day and taking them to the lab for testing. He was diligent about his job, was never in a hurry, and liked to talk to us as he carefully packed away the specimens in a refrigerated container. One afternoon, he related how one of his co-workers had gotten his hair cut while he was making his rounds. His boss found out about it, and Sam related the following conversation:

"Do you mean to say that you got your hair cut on company time?"
"Yes, sir, I did."
"Don't you think that was cheating the company?"
"Well, no, sir. Since my hair grew on company time, I thought it would be all right to get it cut on company time."

"Well, it certainly didn't all grow on company time, did it?"

"No, sir, and I didn't get it all cut off either."

Now, whether this was a true story, I can't say, but as my college English teacher once said, "Never sacrifice a good story for the truth!"

Unimpressed

Because of her very poor vision, Sara had a clock that not only showed the time in large numbers, but spoke the time when a button was pushed. Once I was asked to see her in the nursing home where she lived and diagnosed her with pneumonia. She and I got along famously, but she was not happy with the nursing staff in the home, feeling that they were not attending to her needs very well. She left no doubt as to how she felt about it, and after briefing me thoroughly on the perceived deficiencies, she proceeded to demonstrate the clock, which I had not seen before. I said, "Sara, I'm really impressed with your fancy clock."

Without hesitation, she snapped, "That's good, because the only things that impress me here are you and this clock!"

I Don't Have a Chest

Cliate was an eighty-seven-year-old man who came to see me because of a viral respiratory infection manifest by tightness in his chest. I asked him if he had a poltice at home. He said that he didn't, but could have his family get one for him. I told him to get a mustard plaster and to put it on his chest. He said, "You know, I don't have a chest anymore, can I just put it on the trunk by my bed?"

The Veterinarian

I have been taking care of Boyd for many years, but had never seen his wife. She did come to the office one day for a respiratory infection, and I took care of the problem without too much difficulty. As I walked them out to the front desk, I was talking to him as she paid the bill. She came over to where we were standing and handed Boyd the bill. He glanced at it and exclaimed, "Twenty-five dollars! Why, Doc, that's more than the vet charged me to treat my old cow!" I was glad that his wife laughed, because he sounded awful serious.

Heaven

In the days before tobacco was totally banned from healthcare facilities, I hospitalized an eighty-three-year-old woman from the Nebo area of Bland County. She was truly backwoods, even down to the powdered snuff she constantly had packed away in her buccal pouch, the space between the cheek and the gum. When making rounds on her one day, I said, "Miss Ruth, dipping is such a nasty habit; you need to quit."

She said, "It ain't nasty iffen you don't drool and don't spill it all over you! See here, you just take a little pinch, rare back like this and…" she demonstrated by tilting her head back, pulling out her lower lip and whopping in a goodly-sized "pinch" of the vile stuff. She savored whatever snuff dippers savor, and said, "This is such a good place. I got a clean bed, they fetch me three meals a day, I got a catheter so's I don't hafta get outta bed to pee, they keep my snuff right here on this here tray, they give me a cup to spit in and when it's full, they come an take it away and give me a new one. I hope I never have to go home."

"Wow," I thought, "what more could anyone want?"

Miss Ruth died a few days later…straight from one heaven to another!

Talking to Yourself?

Having a Dr. Booker son can pose some consternation at times. When Jake was practicing in Forest, Virginia, I called one day and told the receptionist, "This is Dr. Booker. May I speak with Dr. Booker?" Without missing a beat, she said, "So, you want to start talking to yourself, do you?"

Later, when he had moved to Winter Haven, Florida, I called him one day and when the receptionist answered, I said, "This is Dr. Booker, may…" but before I could get out another word, she snapped,

"You are most certainly NOT Dr. Booker!"

Sensing an opportunity, I said, "Yes, I am; I just have a cold."

Huffily, she said, "You may have a cold, but you aren't Dr. Booker.

I thought that she might hang up on me so I said as quickly as possible, "This is the Dr. Booker who is your Dr. Booker's father."

A long pause ensued, and then the apologies began. I'm disappointed that I have not been able to trick her again!

Burial Plots

This is not, strictly speaking, medical humor, but brought to me by a patient who had cut it out of the local weekly newspaper:

FOR SALE—Two burial plots in the mausoleum
at Sunset Gardens and window
air conditioner.

Diets

I hear a lot about diets. Diets have never worked to reduce weight, and they will never work, but patients talk ceaselessly about their diets, sometimes serious, and sometimes not so serious. The following are a few one-liners about diets:

The Light Diet—when it gets light, I start eating.

The Seafood Diet—when I see food, I eat it.

Two diets—I'm on two diets, because I don't get enough to eat on one.

Cookie Diet—if you eat enough cookies, it takes away your appetite.

I Never Missed Anything

Miss Evelyn was a delightful elderly lady whose presence seemed to justify more familiarity than "Mrs. Taylor," but less than "Evelyn." According to the tradition of the south, I called her "Miss Evelyn."

To my surprise, she snapped, "Don't call me Miss Evelyn!"

Puzzled, I asked her why she objected to such a time honored salutation.

She grinned and said, "Because they might put that on my tombstone, and I want you to know, I never missed anything!"

The Orkin Man

Ruth had a lot of swelling in her legs. Not wanting to put her on a diuretic, I prescribed a special type of knee-length hose to keep the swelling down. They were very tight, and she had trouble getting them on in the morning. She was complaining to me about her difficulty and said, "Why, just this morning, I had to get the Orkin Man to help me get them on."

Just Call Me Professor

Claude Bruce was a ninety-year-old man who held a Ph.D. in physics and had taught at Tennessee Tech for many years. He retired to Wythe County, and I became his physician. On one occasion, I hospitalized him for pneumonia and always referred to him as Dr. Bruce. One day, he objected to that address and wanted me to call him "mister." I thought that we needed to recognize his education, especially in the rigorous field of physics, and said that "Mister" was just not appropriate.

After a few moment of thought, he said, "Well, how about calling me 'Professor'?" which we did for the rest of our encounters.

Side Effects

Blake had been to see another physician for a respiratory problem and had been given some sample medicine. The physician told him that it might have "side effects" and when Blake came to see me, it was because the admonition had come true, he was having "side" pain. The "side effect/side pain," however, turned out to be a pulled muscle!

A Clothespin

Miss Alta was an elderly woman who began to have trouble with urinary incontinence. In those days, there was little that could be done about the condition, although today there are a number of alternatives. She told me that her brother, with whom she lived, had a similar problem, but she noted that with him it was not much bother, "He just uses a clothespin."

Twenty Seconds

Mr. Henderson, a seventy-six-year-old man with lung disease and poor exercise tolerance told me, "Doctor, I've always been able to whip my weight in tigers; only now I have to get it done in twenty seconds."

Pall Bearers

Mr. Hounshell always wore a flannel shirt under his bib overalls, and going to a funeral was reason enough to get a new shirt and overalls. When the funeral director asked him why he was so dressed up, Mr. Hounshell replied, "Well, I thought, maybe, you might need another 'ball bearer'."

Della told me that one of her neighbors had died, and that two of her brothers had been asked to be the "polar bears."

Gotta Get Another Doctor

I am a stickler about healthy life styles and fitness and rarely lose an opportunity to instruct my patients in the benefits of such. One day, after I had given John the standard lecture, he appeared in the fitness center where I was tearing along on the treadmill. He stopped and looked glumly at me for a second or two and said, "I gotta find another doctor. I want one who smokes, drinks, eats fast food, and is fat." With that he got laboriously on a treadmill and started walking. I figured that, at least in one instance, I had made a difference!

Inflation

Medicine has changed dramatically in the thirty-five years that I have been in practice in Wytheville. The knowledge base and the technology have simply exploded, as have the costs associated with the delivery of that care. In fact, the knowledge and technology factors have increased much more dramatically than the cost of the delivery. As we physicians face the future we must deal with an extremely complex medical system that is disjointed and paradoxical. We are constrained by a burdensome legal system, a government that imposes rules and regulations but is reluctant to pay for the care it dictates, and by insurance companies who, in effect, dictate how we practice medicine. But despite all of the trials and tribulations of practicing medicine today, if we focus on the real reason we do this, medicine is still a rewarding and satisfying profession, made more interesting as we look backward in time. Simpler times demanded simpler fee schedules, and I have run across two early fees schedules, one from the Northern Neck (of Virginia) Medical Association "fee table" adopted in 1907 and a table of fees "as agreed upon by the Caroline County (Virginia) Medical Society in its session of May 25, 1915." Even when Jim Stone and I joined Walter Barton in July 1973, the office call was only $4.00! Today, there are multiple levels of charges depending on the complexity of the problem, the time spent with the patient, the amount of documentation necessary, and any ancillary counseling necessary, but the "office call" in 1907 and 1915 is now what the computer recognizes as 99213 and is $90.00. For comparison, comparable physician obstetrical fees for an uncomplicated delivery are $2,695.00. As you read over these tables, and then compare hospital obstetrical fees from 1950 with today, you will find the humor in this section; you'll have to laugh or else you'll cry!

FEE TABLE
Adopted by the
Northern Neck Medical Association

Office calls..$.50
Extra cases in same house..$.50
Call visits..$1.00
Regular visits...$2.00
Night visits..$4.00
Consultation (first visit)..$5.00
Gonorrhea. Diagnosing and prescribing..........................$1.00
Syphilis. Diagnosing and prescribing..............................$1.00
Minor dislocations, fractures and amputations
       (Greater in proportion).......................................$5.00
Normal obstetric care...$10.00

    It is expressly understood that the above are minimal charges, but shall be greater with the discretion of the physician in charge.

                         J. W. Tankard, President

Ro. O. Lyell, Secretary

Minimun fees as agreed upon by the
Caroline County (Virginia) Medical Society
in its session of May 25, 1915

Office call including examination and prescription during the day.......$1.00
Same at night...$2.00
Home call up to seven miles during the day.........................$2.00
Same at night...$5.00
Any distance over seven miles is to be charged at the rate of:
      Twenty-five cents per mile extra during the day
      Fifty cents per mile extra at night
Visit in a village by a physician residing in the village during the day.........$1.00
Same at night...$2.00
Call visit on the way..$1.00
Night spent in the home of a patient, with rest.......................$5.00
Same, without rest...$10.00
Uncomplicated labor/delivery including 2 extra visits during the day...........$15.00
Same at night...$20.00
      Extra charge for protracted, complicated, or instrument delivery
      Left to the discretion of the attending physician.
Delivery of the placenta during the day................................$5.00
Same at night...$7.50
Smallpox vaccination..$.50
      These fees are binding only when in competition with other
members of this Society.

The schedules above are for office-based practice. For a comparison of hospital cost inflation, consider this bill for obstetrical services from St. Joseph's Hospital in Lancaster, Pennsylvania in October 1950.

Lancaster, Pa., ___10-18___ 19_50_

ST. JOSEPH'S HOSPITAL

Mrs. Carmella E. Barr

R-339

STATEMENTS RENDERED AND PAYABLE WEEKLY

Board:		
9 days, from 10-9 to 10-18 @ $ 6.50 per day	58	50
Operating Room	15	00
Anesthesia	10	00
Xray		
Laboratory	5	00
Medications		65
Bassinette x Nursery—8 days	8	00
Glucose		
Electrocardiogram		
Basal Metabolism Rate		
Blood Transfusions:		
Typings		
Rh Factor		
Cross Matchings		
Plasma		
Physiotherapy		
Ambulance		
Telephone toll call		17
Total	97	32

PLEASE PRESENT STATEMENT WITH REMITTANCE

Obstetrical care has changed dramatically since 1950, and most moms and babies are out of the hospital in two or three days if there are no complications, but for comparison, in 2008 the same care rendered above including delivery, nine days of care for the mother and eight days of care for the baby would cost $20,700.00!

For sooth, we have come a long way, baby!

Nurses

No one understands the role that nurses play in the lives of physicians better than physicians themselves. They are truly our "right hands," and are helpmates beyond compare. I have been fortunate to have had several excellent office nurses, and I am sure that I have been kept out of a lot of trouble by their diligence and oversight. My nurse for the last ten years, Robin Dalton, has been of immeasurable help in this age of computers, diagnostic codes, laboratory codes, and the bane of my existence, the pre-authorization of medications by insurance companies and the authorization of imaging tests by those same functionaries.

In addition to the office nurses, nurses in the hospital are also undercover angels, keeping us abreast of patients' conditions when we are not present. Many's the time I have intervened critically in a patient's care because of the expertise of the nurse on duty calling and telling me of a change in condition and usually saying, "I think you need to come in and see this patient."

As I have indicated elsewhere, nurses have added greatly to my trove of humorous stories and events. Some of these stories have been written elsewhere, but this section is to include other miscellaneous anecdotes provided by nurses over the years.

A Horse's Butt

Freda, an intensive-care unit nurse, was married to a Methodist minister. They raised horses and had a mare that was ready to deliver at any time. Freda, being the more medically inclined of the two, was diligently watching the mare and frequently checked her progress by raising the mare's tail. The pasture was next to a busy thoroughfare, and her husband said, "Freda, we're standing out here in this field right next to the road with people driving by all the time. You can't just stand out here looking at that horse's butt like that."

Freda calmly replied, "Nobody will care. They know I've been married to one for twenty-one years!"

Tie Me Kangaroo Down

Freda, of the above anecdote, was taking care of a ninety-three-year-old man in the intensive-care unit when he became very agitated and restless and was in danger of injuring himself because of his thrashing around. Not wanting to oversedate him with drugs, she placed him in wrist restraints until the dose of anti-anxiety drugs took effect. As she secured the straps to the bedrail, he beckoned her over and whispered, "Do you tie all of your men down like this?"

Just For You

Mrs. Johnson was ninety-five years old and had been admitted to the hospital for ulcer disease. I had started her on some intravenous medicine that resulted in her becoming wildly agitated, and it took three nurses to keep her in the bed. Fran asked her, "Mrs. Johnson, did you fight like this when you were younger?"

"No," she replied, "I saved it all up for you!"

Frances Times Two

Frances is a nurse who has retired and unretired so many times she thinks she's caught in a revolving door. Once when she was fretting over a very ill patient she told me that she didn't know why she was worrying so. "You know" she said, "worry is like being in a rocking chair...it gives you something to do, but it doesn't get you anywhere, so I'm turning the worrying over to you."

Another time when I came on the floor, Frances greeted me with the news that three of the patients on the floor had died on her shift.

Mrs. Russell had been the first to go, then Mr. Rouse had died, and finally Mr. Rielly had just passed away. Frances shook her head and said, "The only good thing I can find is that God is calling us in reverse alphabetical order today!"

Take Care of Her

Patsy Muncy is a registered nurse and nursing instructor in the local community college. She cut her teeth as a nurse in the intensive-care unit at our hospital and has supplied me with a number of funny stories as we spent time together taking care of critically ill patients. One night she told me that her grandmother was in a nursing home and, being confused much of the time, she spent much time talking to the deities. On one of Patsy's visits, her grandmother took her hand, looked skyward, and said, "Jesus, this one is not as smart as the rest, but she does come to see me, so take good care of her."

Just Hold Me

Jettie was helping ninety-six-year-old John McGee from the toilet back to bed when he stopped and said, "Lady, I know it's not gentlemanly, but could I hold you for a time?" Jettie, being a fine southern woman, stopped right there and put her arms out to him. Mr. McGee wrapped his spindly old arms around her for a few seconds and went on back to bed saying, "Thank you, ma'am. It's been so long since I held a woman!"

Pain in the Rear

Mary Ann Fields, my nurse of many years ago in the dark ages of paper charts, was diligent in always putting a notation of the patient's complaint on the top of the chart, so that I would have some idea of the problem before I went into the room. One morning I picked up the chart on an elderly, very proper lady to find "Rear pain" as the chief complaint. I sat down at the desk, and after exchanging a few pleasantries, I said, "So you have a problem with your rear today?"

She fixed me with a stony stare and icily replied, "Doctor, I have a pain in my right ear!" From then on, I made sure that Mary Ann adequately separated the abbreviations for right and left from the rest of the complaint!

Taking No Chances

When one of Larry's patients, a young Baptist minister, asked, "Are you saved, brother Larry?" he replied, "Why, hell yes, Reverend; I ain't taking no damned chances!"

Why the Blood?

At our old office, we had no conference room and had to conduct non-medical business in an empty examining room. On this day a young woman had come in to interview for a nursing position. She was put in one of Walt Barton's rooms, and Jim Stone and I interviewed her first and felt that she would be a good person to hire. Walt was made aware of our feelings and went in, determined to make a good impression and using his most professional bearing, he ended the interview by asking, "Is there anything you would like to know?"

She replied, "Well, there's nothing about the job itself, but why did I have to have blood drawn?" Well, Walt was stunned into speechlessness, stammered a little, but right away, he figured, correctly as it turned out, that the lab tech had been directed to the wrong room! As he tried gracefully to get out of a tight spot, the lady obviously had guessed the error and said, "You know, I've been treated and I haven't given anybody syphilis for years!" The tension eased, and we went on to hire her, deciding that anyone who could be that quick was worth having as a nurse.

The Laugh's on Me

Two Brains

Many years ago, Dr. Jim Stone had an elderly patient who had a very strange and unsettling affect which was apparent to everyone who knew her. She had advanced blood vessel disease of the brain, and had suffered several strokes, one of which resulted in blindness. She said, over and over, that she could see nothing at all; her vision was totally black. Indeed, she certainly appeared to be blind, and her husband had to do all of the housework and lead her wherever they went. And yet, if you approached her and stuck out your hand, she would unerringly shake hands with you. Also, at times, if something would fall near her, she would try to catch it, and at times, she also seemed to recognize faces or expressions. When these things were pointed out to her, she seemed puzzled, and could not explain why she reacted in such a fashion; she insisted that everything looked black.

She had been seen by neurologists who felt that the condition was due to the stroke, since brain scans showed that damage had occurred in the visual cortex, but they went no further in explanation. Most of us felt that, even if she was not malingering, she was certainly taking advantage of her husband's good nature, as he assumed all of the household duties, and patiently cared for her until her death.

It was not until I was reading the April 9, 2007 issue of *Newsweek* magazine that enlightenment finally struck. Neuroscience has progressed to the point that the structure of the brain is much better understood, and this article expounded on what was called "our messy, reptilian brains." Over millions of years of human evolution, our brains have added multiple layers of sophistication, but primitive structures still underlie all of that. Accordingly, we have two separate visual systems, one based in the midbrain and the other in the visual cortex of the brain. The *Newsweek* article succinctly explained our patient's situation.

"Just as the mouse brain is a lizard brain…the human brain is essentially a mouse brain with extra toppings. That's how we wound up with two visual systems. In amphibians, signals from the eye are processed in a region called the midbrain, which, for instance, guides a frog's tongue to insects in midair and enables us to duck as an errant fastball bears down on us. Our kludgy brain retains this primitive visual structure even though most signals from the eye are processed in the visual cortex, a newer addition. If the latter is damaged, patients typically say they cannot see a thing. Yet if asked to reach for an object, many of them can grab it on the first try. And if asked to judge the emotional expression on a face, they get it right more often than chance would predict—especially if that expression is anger.

"They are not lying about being unable to see. In such "blindsight," people who have lost what most of us think of as vision are seeing with the amphibian visual system. But because the midbrain is not connected to higher cognitive regions, they have no conscious awareness of an object's location or a face's expression. Consciously, the world looks inky black. But, unconsciously, signals from the midbrain are merrily zipping along to the amygdala (which assesses emotion) and the motor cortex (which makes the arm reach out)."

As this information hit home, I could not wait to tell Jim, so I took the article it into his office and sat watching his expression as he read it. He immediately recognized the relationship to our patient, and when he looked back at me all he said was, "Well, I'll be damned!"

A Neurological Deficit

Tim came to the office for a cold. It seemed to be straight forward, but when I asked him to open his mouth his tongue fell over to the left side. I looked all around, but could not see any abnormality, so I had him close his mouth and open again. Again the tongue flopped over to the left side. This repeated a third time and puzzled, I asked, "Tim, does your tongue always deviate to the left when you open your mouth?"

He grinned and said, "Only when I want to keep my gum from falling out!"

All for Cynthia

Bob was in the office with a bad case of hives. When I questioned him about a possible cause he said that it had started when he was trimming for Cynthia. When I asked him what kind of bush he was trimming for her, he looked a little puzzled, and then the light dawned. "No, Doctor," he said, "I was trimming..." and he said this very slowly, "forsythia."

Mattie

Mattie was an elderly lady from Max Meadows, Virginia, which is just up I-81 from Wytheville. She had delivered 11 babies, 10 of them at home, and had 7 living children at the time I took care of her. She came to see me one day because she felt that her face had been "twitching." The exchange went like this:

"My face has been twitching and drawing, and I need something done."

"Mattie, I can't see anything at all. Where do you feel it?"

"Well, it's right there in front of you, can't you see it?"

"No, ma'am, I don't see a thing."

"Well, get up a little closer."

I did.

"See it now?"

"No, I can't."

"Maybe if you get a magnifying glass you can see it."

So I got a magnifying glass and searched the affected area without seeing anything, but to appease her, I said, "Well, now, I think I did see a little twitch."

"Well," she said, "that's funny, nobody else can see it!"

Oh, My God!

Barbara is very health conscious and sees me annually for preventive care. Following a recent complete physical exam, I left the room and attended to several other matters before I went back. I thought I had given her ample time to dress and did not bother to knock, but when I opened the door, she was still undressed. With an exclamation of surprise, I quickly closed the door.

Before entering the room again, I had Robin precede me to be sure she was fully dressed. As we went into the room, Barbara said, "Well, doctor, you sure know how to make a lady feel good! You see me completely naked, and all you can say is, 'Oh, my God, Barbara!'"

Our laughter eased my embarrassment considerably.

In Closing

"There are more things in heaven and earth, Horatio,
than are dreamt of in our philosophy."
—Shakespeare

This chapter is not so much humorous as it is fascinating. In 1968, the *National Observer* newspaper published an article about people near death having an unusual experience of leaving their bodies, but being fully cognizant of all that was happening to them. The article described them as "hovering" over their bodies, yet being able to see and hear all that was going on, but incapable of making themselves seen or heard. Many of my medical school classmates read the article, and we adopted the term "hovering" when referring to patients who were near death. To say a patient was "hovering" conveyed all that needed to be said about the seriousness of their condition. Then, in 1970, Dr. Raymond Moody published his book *Life After Life,* describing in detail many examples of what he called "near-death experiences," a term that has become widely accepted as descriptive of the experience. In true near-death experiences, the people not only leave their bodies, they pass through a tunnel, come into the presence of a glowing Being of Light, experience a review of their lives, and are then returned to their earthly existence. During the experience, the people are enthralled by the beauty, peace, and sense of complete love and acceptance by the Being of Light, and they are reluctant to return to their former lives. The subject captured my interest, and I have become a student of the phenomenon ever since. It remains one of the most fascinating of all human experiences, and I have used my knowledge of it extensively in my day-to-day practice. I am also more aware of the possibility of critically-ill patients having such an event, but it always surprises me, as indicated by the story below.

Your Ugly Face

Mrs. Johnson was Dr. Barton's patient in the intensive care unit, having had a heart attack. I was making rounds in the unit one morning when she suddenly went into cardiac arrest. The nurses and I went immediately into her room and were able to resuscitate her very quickly. She was stable, but groggy, after the event, and I went back to my charting. Later I went back to see her. Upon recognizing me, she was very angry. She told me to get away from her; she did not want to see me or talk to me. Puzzled over her reaction, I left the room, and continued my rounds in the hospital. I could not get over her response, and I soon went back to see her. She turned her back to me, obviously still upset. "Mrs. Johnson," I said, "I don't understand why you are so angry with me. Your heart stopped beating. You were nearly dead, and I got you going again, I would think that you would be glad."

She turned over, fixed me with a furious stare and said, "That's just the point, Doctor. There I was in the most beautiful place you can imagine and the next thing I knew, I woke up back here looking up at your ugly face!" Suddenly it hit me; Miss Johnson had just had a near-death experience! With time, she came to accept that I was not the vehicle of her return; it was just not her time to go. And although we settled into a friendly relationship, she never let me forget about being jerked out of heaven!

An Angel

Although I have had many patients who have had near-death experiences, patients with other paranormal phenomena are just as fascinating. Fred was an elderly man under my care when he developed symptoms of an abscess in his abdomen. It appeared that he would need surgery, and he was frightened beyond reason that he would not survive an operative procedure. He became restless and agitated, and nothing I could say would placate him. Finally one morning I went into his room to find him completely at ease, cheerful, and eating breakfast. Nothing physically had changed, and I was amazed at the change in him. I told him that I was glad that he was so much better and asked him if he knew why. "Dr. Booker, I had a visitor last night," he said, and I immediately thought that a minister had done more than I would have thought possible. My thought was quickly dispelled when he related the rest of the story. He had been sleeping when he became aware of someone in the room at the end of his bed. He described the visitor as appearing "bright white and kind of shining." "He was just looking at me and smiling. I thought he was a nurse, but he didn't say anything at all, he just stood there. But, doctor, the most amazing thing happened; he somehow showed me that whatever happens, now or later, is okay, and I am going to be all right. I rubbed my eyes, and when I opened them again, he was gone, but you know, I am fine now. You can do anything you have to do to get me well." Fred lived for many more years and never once did he ever again appear frightened about the prospect of his death.

Another Angel

Mr. Robert Catron came under my care when he was found to have acute leukemia. He was elderly, and after a long siege of therapy at the National Institutes of Health, he elected to take no further treatment and just wanted comfort and supportive care. This was before the age of hospice services, and I became the source of his terminal care. He developed pneumonia and, to make him as comfortable as possible, I hospitalized him. After a few days, he realized that the end was near and became extremely frightened. He was agitated and restless, could not eat, and was constantly nauseated. I gave him sedatives, but they did little to control the underlying condition. One morning on rounds, I found him dramatically improved. He was sitting up in bed eating and was as calm as a cucumber. When I commented on the change, he said, "I had a visitor last night. It was like a shining blue light over there in the corner. I couldn't make out if it was a man or a woman, but whoever it was made me feel wonderful, and I know that everything is going to be alright. You know, I think it was an angel." Like Fred's had, his fear disappeared, and he died in peace several days later.

Hello from Heaven

The title for this anecdote is actually the title of a book written by William Guggenheim, in which he discusses the frequent occurrence of people being contacted in some way by a recently deceased loved one. These contacts may be visual, auditory, tactile, or psychological, but even though these occurrences are reassuring, they are both surprising and confounding. The following story was related to me by Betty, whose mother had died several years before her father. Several months after her mother's death, Betty was vacuuming the living room when she sensed a presence in the room. She looked around, and saw her mother sitting on the sofa, smiling at her and looking very peaceful. Betty was astounded, and just stood there briefly without saying anything, but when she started toward the sofa, her mother just faded from sight. This same thing occurred several times over the next few months, and Betty even began to anticipate and enjoy the visits though there were never any words spoken.

Later when her father died, Betty felt that she would not see her mother's image again, but she was wrong. Several weeks after her father's funeral, she was in the living room cleaning and straightening when she, once again, felt the strange presence and, looking toward the sofa, she saw both her mother and her father sitting side by side, smiling at her and at each other. Again, though no words were spoken, Betty was given the message that mom and dad were together again and would not return. In a few moments they faded away together and, indeed, Betty never saw them again.

An Angel for Brian

"Dear Brian,

Your graduation announcement was a very special encouragement to me. I will never forget the little red-headed kid who accidentally hung himself on the clothesline. I'll never forget how desperately hopeless I felt when I first saw you in the emergency room that night. I remember discussing your accident with the pediatric neurologist in Roanoke and getting absolutely no encouragement about your life and about your ability to function if you survived. I remember sitting down with your parents and Pastor Smith in the intensive care waiting room and praying for you....

Your story is one that I have told frequently because I think it's important for us to be reminded that while our personal resources are limited when we seek to treat people, God's resources are never limited, and He is the one who should ultimately get credit for any healing.

Thanks so much for sending the announcement. Although I would never have forgotten you without the announcement, it was good to be reminded of your achievement and of God's goodness to us.

Your friend and former family doctor,
Dean Patton, M.D."

This letter was given to me by Jean Shultz, Brian's mother, after she told me of the amazing recovery made by Brian that day. Brian had wanted to take a rope up in a tree so he could tie it to a limb and swing down. To free his hands for climbing, he had tied it around his neck, but as he started up the tree, he fell, with the rope being caught by a limb, and he hung by his neck for an unknown length of time. When he was discovered, he was lifeless, and in the emergency room, his death was felt to be imminent. Later, in the intensive-care unit, he was pronounced dead. This is the situation described by Dr. Patton in his letter. Amazingly, Brian recovered completely and now leads a normal life.

There are several other interesting things about this case which make it appropriate for this chapter. First, though he did not tell anyone for several months after the episode, Brian recalled being cradled in a warm and loving bright light and "talking to God," and this has had a profound effect on his life ever since. Second, Jean and Danny, Brian's father, vividly remember a pretty nurse who came to the waiting room frequently during Brian's stay in the intensive care unit. She repeatedly told them that Brian was "going to be fine," despite all of the dire prognostications by Dr. Patton and the pediatric neurologist. Although Jean was dubious about the opinion of a nurse, she was very comforted by her kind and encouraging words and wrote down her name. After Brian had recovered, Jean went back to the hospital to look up the nurse to thank her for all she had done. Even though her visit was shortly after the incident, no one at the hospital knew this nurse, and the hospital had no record of anyone by that name or position working, or having ever worked at the hospital!

"There are more things in heaven and earth…."

Last Thoughts

In times of stress and sorrow
Humor will brighten up your day.
It will lighten all your burdens
And drive the blues away.

In youthfulness and vigor,
Humor is easy enough to find.
It hovers everywhere
And comes easily to your mind.

But life is not always easy,
And when with illness you are beset,
Humor becomes difficult to see
And much easier to forget.

Illness, anxiety, and sorrow
May fall into your way,
And you are left to wonder
"Where's life so bright and gay?"

But if you can remember
To keep humor in your life,
Your health will be much better,
And you will suffer much less strife.

So look you ever upward
To the source of joy sublime.
God's humor will carry you onward
Until you reach that world divine.

Also available from PublishAmerica

EDUCATING ANDREW
By Virginia Lanier Biasotto

The strongest bond in the animal kingdom is mother and offspring.

When something threatens, the mother instinctively acts to protect. The story of Andrew is a human example, and the enemy was one of our most revered institutions: the public school.

For most children, the beginning of school is a time of anticipation and excitement. New clothes and supplies are purchased. A preliminary visit to the classroom sets the stage for the promise, "This is where you will learn to read." For Andrew, the reading part didn't happen. For seven years solutions were sought, found and rejected. The printed page remained a mystery. The effects of his failure to read were dire. Andrew's love of life had been taken away, and his parents and teachers were helpless to do anything about it.

Paperback, 132 pages
5.5" x 8.5"
ISBN 1-4241-0171-9

When it appeared that Andrew would remain illiterate as he entered junior high school, a door opened that would change his life and that of his mother forever.

About the author:

VIRGINIA (GINGER) LANIER BIASOTTO is a native of Delaware and a graduate of the University of Delaware (1959). She is the founder of Reading ASSIST® Institute and the author of ten Reading ASSIST® text books. In 2005, Virginia received Delaware's Jefferson Award for Public Service for her contribution to literacy. She and her husband, Lawrence, are semi-retired and spend half of each year in Wilmington, Delaware, close to children, grandchildren and mothers, and the other half in Palm City, Florida.

Available to all bookstores nationwide.
www.publishamerica.com

Also available from PublishAmerica

RETURN TO THE ASHAU
By John James Kielty

A most secret plan by the U.S. Government to prepare for a pullout from Vietnam was initiated in 1968 just after the momentous Tet Offensive. The plan called for the caching of great treasure to support the expected network of spies that would stay behind. The Green Beret soldiers who unknowingly planted these treasure troves learned of its existence and now they were determined to retrieve it. The officials who directed these missions in the past were now holding higher offices and were ambitiously seeking even higher positions. The American public could not be allowed to find out about the government's plan to cut and run and the needless deaths of thousands of our young men and women who fought and died for a cause already determined to be without merit.

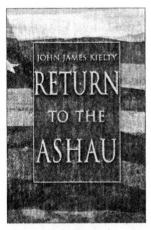

Paperback, 358 pages
6" x 9"
ISBN 1-4241-2124-8

When these government officials learn of the covert plans of these men to retrieve this treasure, they decide this cannot occur and the deadly decisions are made. The chase begins and with it the treachery and lies.

About the author:

John James Kielty spent twenty years as a warrior soldier, or as the Irish would call him, one of the Wild Geese. Though born in Ireland, he fought in America's wars proudly and with distinction. John James Kielty is proud of the great heritage of Irish writers with whom he shares a love of the written word. He now lives in semi-retirement in the rural mountains of southern West Virginia that are so much like his native Ireland in appearance. He spends his free time working with wood and periodically sitting at his keyboard.

Available to all bookstores nationwide.
www.publishamerica.com

Also available from PublishAmerica

THE SEED OF OMEGA
By Eugene Ettlinger

The Seed of Omega depicts the molding of
rural Palestine from the windblown nomadic
land of weeds and sand into a Mecca in the
Middle East. The land was populated by
assimilation through different cultures, which
includes an ethnic invasion after the soil had
been tilled. A greater understanding of
political power through favored in-migration
status shows the melding of a select society.
The power brokers governing the land
became subservient to the will of neighboring
nations in exchange for the production of
oil. The cast is composed of variations of
the Middle Eastern Arab people, the power
brokers of the British Empire and the exiles
from hostile nations the world over.

Paperback, 511 pages
6" x 9"

ISBN 1-4137-8882-3

The diversity of characters represents
different walks of life to be filled by the shoes
of the reader. They fought for survival and a love for one another. They
were dedicated to the building of a society while struggling to implement a
diverse nation running from a past life simply to find a place in which to be.
Their fears are offset by the courage to survive in the creation of a nation.

About the author:

A native New Yorker and Fordham University graduate,
Gene Ettlinger performed graduate studies in the field of
sociology. Gene's dedication is in the development of
community life. Growing up in the mixing bowl of ethnic
diversity led to his keen interest in the alienation of unskilled
workers. Gene is a pilot, skier, skilled boating enthusiast,
and an accomplished artist. He currently resides in New
York and Florida.

Available to all bookstores nationwide.
www.publishamerica.com

Also available from PublishAmerica

SIOBHAN
An AI's Adventure
By Emma L. Haynes

Siobhan: An AI's Adventure is a story
that follows an android from his creation
to his death. His most important mission
is to pilot a colony ship filled with one
hundred humans to a new planet, where
he is to become a simple computer. A
colonist tries to kill Siobhan before they
land at their destination. This disruption
causes the colony ship to shoot past the
desired planet and crash land on a planet
of an advanced race. Siobhan and only
three humans survive. Fighting off attacks
from the locals, Siobhan gets them off the
planet.

Paperback, 176 pages
5.5" x 8.5"
ISBN 978-1-60749-130-9

About the author:

Emma L. Haynes lives in North Pole, Alaska. She is married to an
Army soldier and has one son. Through the years, she has enjoyed
writing poetry, science fiction, fantasy, and historical fiction. She plans
to travel the world when she gets the chance. She has one book
published entitled *Poems from the Heart*. Visit her website at
www.EmmaLHaynes.com.

Available to all bookstores nationwide.
www.publishamerica.com